THE NEW EVANGELIZATION AND YOU

The New Evangelization and You

Be Not Afraid

GREG WILLITS

PUBLISHED BY FRANCISCAN MEDIA
Cincinnati, Ohio

Unless otherwise noted, Scripture passages have been taken from the *Revised Standard Version*, Catholic edition. Copyright 1946, 1952, 1971 by the Division of Christian Education of the National Council of Churches of Christ in the USA. Used by permission. All rights reserved.

Quotes are taken from the English translation of the *Catechism of the Catholic Church* for the United States of America (indicated as CCC), 2nd ed. Copyright 1997 by United States Catholic Conference —Libreria Editrice Vaticana.

Cover design by Candle Light Studios
Cover image © Studio-Annika
Book design by Mark Sullivan

LIBRARY OF CONGRESS CATALOGING-IN-PUBLICATION DATA
Willits, Greg.
The new evangelization and you : be not afraid / Greg Willits.
pages cm
Includes bibliographical references (p.   ) and index.
ISBN 978-1-61636-515-8 (alk. paper)
1. Catholic Church—Missions. 2. Evangelistic work—Catholic Church.
3. Catholic Church—Doctrines. I. Title.
BV2180.W53 2013
269'.2—dc23
2013002737

ISBN 978-1-61636-515-8

Published by Servant Books, an imprint of Franciscan Media.
28 W. Liberty St.
Cincinnati, OH 45202
www.FranciscanMedia.org

Printed in the United States of America.
Printed on acid-free paper.
13 14 15 16 17 5 4 3 2 1

To Mom and Dad,
who evangelized most loudly
by their silent weekend mornings,
drinking coffee and reading their Bibles.

Contents

Foreword

The year was 1770, and in a small Italian church, two altar boys prepared for Benediction. Annibale Della Genga and Francesco Castiglioni entered the sacristy, put on their albs, and grabbed the heavy brass candlesticks. And then they began to bicker.

Arguing over who would stand on the priest's right for the procession, their quibble escalated into a shouting match. Alarmed parishioners turned their heads to the back of the church to see the commotion, and that's when it happened:

Castiglioni cracked Della Genga over the head with his candlestick.

Blood dripped out of Della Genga's head, and both boys began shoving each other. Shocked parishioners screamed, "Throw them out! Throw them out!" So the embarrassed priest grabbed the boys, led them to the door, and tossed them out of the church.

Fast-forward several decades to 1825. Half a million people gathered in Rome for the great Jubilee celebration. The Jubilee occurs every twenty-five years, and its grand climax is the opening of the Holy Door at St. Peter's Basilica. Traditionally, the pope would knock on the door three times with a large silver hammer and sing, "Open unto me the gates of justice!" On the third knock, the door would swing open, and the pope would lead his people through. The symbolism was rich: pilgrims from all over the world coming back home to the Church, following their leader through the great *porta fidei*, the "door of faith."

This particular Jubilee year, in front of thousands of pilgrims, Cardinal Della Genga made his way to the door. It was fifty-five years after the candlestick incident. Only he was no longer Cardinal Della Genga. He was Pope Leo XII. And as he neared the door, he turned to the cardinal beside him—Cardinal Castiglioni—and said, "Let me have the hammer."

With a sly grin, Castiglioni replied, "Just like I gave you the candlestick?"

Amazingly, four years later Castiglioni succeeded his friend and became pope himself, taking the name Pius VIII.

Now, if you told any of those pew-sitters back in 1770 that they had two future popes in the back of their church, they would have laughed you out of the building, saying, "Those two boys? The ones shoving and whacking each other with candlesticks? You've got to be kidding."

Most of us have a similar reaction whenever we think about evangelization: "Who, me? You can't be serious. How could I be an evangelist? I hardly know my faith. I'm too timid. I'm too awkward. I don't like controversy. I'm the *last* person that should be evangelizing." Compounding these feelings of fear and inadequacy is the problem that many of us have little idea what evangelization *is*, or how to do it.

That's why *The New Evangelization and You* is so timely and refreshing. Greg Willits wipes away confusion, counters our greatest fears, and gives us challenging yet gentle encouragement. Packed with specific, practical advice on evangelizing, this book will not only help you understand what evangelization is but leave you confident in doing it yourself.

You'll especially appreciate his clear threefold path to evangelization: know your faith, live your faith, share your faith. As Pope Benedict has often noted, catechesis—knowing one's faith—is crucial to living and sharing it. It's no accident he launched the Year of Faith alongside the anniversary of the *Catechism of the Catholic Church*. The two are closely linked. Once we grasp what the Church teaches and why, we'll be much more emboldened to share it.

However, as Greg explains, knowing our faith is not enough. We also must also live it by cultivating our prayer life, participating in our parish, and frequenting the sacraments. All of that activity grounds us in God and attunes us to his promptings. Greg is the perfect example of this dynamic. Before taking his faith seriously, he hardly evangelized. Yet after he renewed his commitment to the Lord and the Church, he's become one of the most effective evangelists in America.

Finally, Greg says, we've got to share our faith. Once we know it, once we live it, we're charged with spreading it to others. Catholicism is always personal, but it's never private. As Pope Paul VI wrote in 1975, "The Church exists to evangelize." Spreading the Good News of Jesus risen from the dead is her basic mission—and, thus, ours too.

These three callings—to know, live, and share our faith—have been around since the time of Christ. But most Catholics only practice one or two of them. In recent years, however, a new movement has given them fresh emphasis and form. Pope John Paul II christened it the "New Evangelization" back in 1979. Yet it wasn't until 1983 that he began to unpack it. Speaking to a group of bishops in Haiti, he described the New Evangelization as not a new message, but a new delivery, one that was "new in ardor, methods, and expressions."

If he were still living today, I think Pope John Paul would describe Greg's book the same way (and I think if the pope read Greg's book, Greg would have a heart attack.) As you'll discover, this book bubbles with excitement—with "new ardor." On every page you sense Greg's zeal for the New Evangelization and by the end, you'll share it, too. As longtime readers and radio listeners know, Greg is naturally hilarious (who else can tie the New Evangelization to the six degrees of Kevin Bacon?) He's also a gifted storyteller who is not afraid to share stories of both success and failure. With great candor, charm, and excitement, his book embodies the "new ardor."

Also, Greg's book highlights many "new methods" of evangelizing. Over the years, Greg has used dozens of tools to evangelize. Whether digital forms like Facebook, YouTube, and radio, or decidedly non-digital means like hand-crafted rosaries, he's constantly coming up with fresh ways to spread the faith. In the book, you'll learn the background behind many of his efforts.

However, the book isn't primarily about Greg; it's about *you*. Greg shares his new methods in order to get your mind racing with your own new ideas. He demonstrates that you don't have to trek to a remote African tribe in order to evangelize. If you have a computer, phone, or handful of yarn, you can evangelize right now using new methods of your own.

Finally, Greg's book offers several "new expressions." The New Evangelization is not a one-size-fits-all project; there's no one right way to do it. It demands varied and diverse expressions, and that's what Greg offers here. In addition to his own examples, you'll find profiles of many ordinary Catholics modeling creative ways to do the New Evangelization. They all have normal backgrounds—engineers, stay-at-home moms, entrepreneurs, young priests—but they share their faith in extraordinary ways. As G.K. Chesterton wrote, "The Church is a house with a hundred gates, and no two men enter at exactly the same angle." Here you'll glimpse many of those different angles.

He probably didn't know it when he started writing, but with this book Greg follows in the footsteps of Della Genga and Castiglioni. He doesn't wield any brass candlesticks. He doesn't swing silver hammers (at least not that I know of). But Greg's whole life is aimed at leading people through the *porta fidei*, the door of faith.

Through his writing, speaking, podcasting, and other work, he's helped countless people come home to the Catholic Church. That's what the New Evangelization is all about, and that's exactly what this book will help you do, too.

Brandon Vogt
author of The Church and New Media

Acknowledgments

To those who know me, it goes without saying that pretty much everything I do (or try to do) in Catholic media and ministry, I couldn't do without my wife, Jennifer. She is my support, my absolute best friend, and an incredible source of strength and inspiration. This book only happened because of the times she kicked me out of the house or blockaded the kids from my office and encouraged me in prayer and writing on a topic that is deeply important to both of us. Though she didn't coauthor this book, as she did my first one, *The Catholics Next Door: Adventures in Imperfect Living* (Servant, 2012), what you hold in your hands must be credited in great part to her.

Thanks as well to all of our children—Sam, Walter, Ben, Tommy, and Lily—who have grown up in the shadow of their dad at work on one project or another. They are children of the John Paul II and Pope Benedict XVI generations, and to me they are the reason why the New Evangelization is so very important. They too made sacrifices (even if they weren't aware of them) during the writing of this book, and I pray that the encouragement they have offered may be a witness to other families. I hope and pray that they will continue to seek God's will in their lives. If you would, please keep their future vocations in your prayers.

I would be remiss if I didn't thank the supporters of the various ministries within our NewEvangelizers.com apostolate, as well as our board of directors, board of advisors, and volunteers. Thanks to all of our New Evangelizers bloggers and volunteers, especially Sarah Reinhard, Bryan Murdaugh, Dan Gonzalez, Michael Wojcik, Maria Johnson, Fr. Timothy Gallagher, Lisa Hendey, Patrick Madrid, Fr. Robert Reed, Matt Swaim, Mike Aquilina, and all our friends and supporters in the archdioceses of Atlanta and Denver.

Lastly, thanks to everyone at Franciscan Media for their perseverance and dedication to this project as this book took form over many months. I couldn't be more excited for this project to inspire others to overcome their fears and to become new evangelizers, and the many conversations with everyone at Servant Books and Franciscan Media played a significant role in the direction of this final draft. My appreciation goes out to all of you.

A Short Chapter (Introduction)

My wife and I have had a running joke since before we were married. As long as I can remember, whenever I pick up a new book—whether it is a novel, a textbook, a biography, or even a book in the Bible—I read the introduction. My wife never does. She jumps right to chapter one.

"But if you don't read the introduction," I've protested time and again, "you might be completely missing important material that sets the groundwork for the entire book!"

This never persuades my bride.

"If it was so important, it would be in the main part of the book," she counters.

So for her and all others who skip introductions in books, what you are about to read is *not* an introduction. Instead I'm just calling it "a short chapter." But if you share with me membership in the "Introduction Readers Association," we'll call what you're about to read "the introduction."

Why does this section of the book matter?

Because I want to start this book about the New Evangelization with the point that not every approach to the topic of our faith works the same for everyone else. Catholicism is Catholicism, and the teachings of the Church are rock solid. But not everyone learns the same way. Not everyone lives our faith the same way.

And not everyone shares the faith the same way. Some people read introductions, and some people don't.

Our faith is our faith, and truth is but one truth, but Catholicism draws people to herself in a myriad of ways. I hope this "Short Chapter" or "Introduction" will find some common ground for us all to begin our individual journeys in the New Evangelization.

Time to Burn

Throughout this book I'll reiterate the definition I typically use when attempting to quickly explain—before that glazed look appears in the eyes of whomever I'm speaking to—the New Evangelization: The New Evangelization is about re-evangelizing the world for Jesus Christ, starting with us. It is about knowing the Catholic faith more deeply, living that faith more fully, and sharing the faith more successfully. (Quite honestly, if by the end of this book you're doing any of these things with even a modicum of improvement, I'll consider this work successful.)

While speaking to members of the College of Cardinals about the New Evangelization during a day of reflection in February 2012, Cardinal Timothy Dolan of New York said that the teaching of the Second Vatican Council "refines the Church's understanding of her evangelical duty, defining the entire Church as missionary, that all Christians, by reason of baptism, confirmation, and Eucharist, are evangelizers."[1]

This is important for you to keep in mind. You have a calling. Once the faith is embedded in your brain and propelling your life, the Holy Spirit will work through you to spread the Good News to others. You may not clearly know what that entails at this very moment, but I firmly believe that God desires you to grow in understanding his purpose in your life, especially in relation to the role waiting for you in the New Evangelization. I want to light a fire under you. Or rather, I want to simply inspire *you* to ask the Holy Spirit to light a fire under you.

I want you not only to believe that Catholicism is the greatest part of your life—a golden, shining beacon of hope and truth and faith and joy and constant love—but also to experience a nearly insatiable hunger for knowledge about your faith that draws you on a daily basis to become more excited about its role in your daily existence.

Furthermore, once you're on a daily journey of exploring and growing in the knowledge of your faith, I want you to stoke the fires even hotter, so that you can live your Catholic identity to the fullest. After all, do you want to just be a Catholic who talks the talk, or do you want to be a soldier for our gracious God in heaven who walks the walk?

Last, I want that ongoing thirst for knowledge and that unquenchable desire to live out your faith to be so consuming ("for our God is a consuming fire," Hebrews 12:29 tells us) that it spills out of you and makes it impossible for you to keep it to yourself.

Simply Said

We need to start with a very simple truth: You can be a better Christian.

You're not as good a Christian as you could be or should be, and if you're completely honest with yourself, you'll probably admit that you're not as good a Christian as you *want* to be. I don't care if you've gone to Mass or Christian services every day of your life. It doesn't matter if you read your Bible three hours each morning or pray four rosaries before you get out of bed. It doesn't matter if you're the pope.

You catch that? Even if you're the pope, you can be a better Christian. (Hello, Holy Father, if you're reading this. I love you. Good job you're doing. Pray for me, please.)

We all can be better Christians. And that's OK. Because it's good to have goals. And what better goal is there than eternal happiness with our Father in heaven?

You can do better. I can do better. Everyone in this whole wide world can do better when it comes to living out our Christian faith. And this is at the root of the New Evangelization: constant conversion. We are called to do better because we are called to be witnesses for Jesus Christ in every aspect and at every moment of our lives.

At the onset of the Thirteenth Ordinary General Assembly of the Synod of Bishops, where the focus would be on New Evangelization and the beginning of an exciting Year of Faith in the Catholic Church, Cardinal Donald Wuerl, archbishop of Washington, D.C., and general relator of the synod, made clear a fourfold mission set forward by Pope Benedict XVI to address the New Evangelization. The four points are to

1. reaffirm the essential nature of evangelization;
2. note the theological foundations of the New Evangelization;
3. encourage the many current manifestations of the New Evangelization;
4. suggest practical ways in which the New Evangelization can be encouraged, structured and implemented.[2]

"You shall receive power when the Holy Spirit has come upon you, and you shall be my witnesses in Jerusalem and in all Judea and Samaria, and to the end of the earth" (Acts 1:8).

Have you been a witness for Christ to all around you? Even if you have, you could be doing better.

Don't take this as the scolding of an overbearing parent or a cynical teacher. Take this more from the perspective of your buddy encouraging you at the gym to lift just one more rep or to go five more minutes on the treadmill. Just as a bodybuilder never quite gets to a point of being as strong as he or she wants, a Christian should never be complacent in where he or she is in her faith.

"Come on, man (or woman)! Feel that burn! Push it! Get stronger!"

We can do it. We can be stronger Christians. We can be more loving children of God. We can be better, for God deserves our best. As witnesses, disciples, servants, and leaders, each day is an opportunity to take one step closer to heaven and another step deeper into our relationship with Jesus Christ.

But it's not easy.

The Challenge

There's no denying that we live in a world that oftentimes feels completely messed up. We have an overabundance of wars, political polarizations, quarrels within our own homes and parishes, disrespect for human life in multiple forms, belittling of the message of Christianity, and blatant attacks on religious liberties. Is it even feasible to preach the gospel effectively in today's world?

I say it is. Why would Jesus give us the challenge of witnessing to the ends of the earth if it was a task of pessimistic futility?

I'm convinced that most Christians, even ones who find themselves mired in sinful behavior that may at times seem inescapable, desire a greater closeness with God. Most desire the freedom that comes from being bound not to the ways of this world but to our God.

I'm convinced that many of us hold within our hearts an almost insatiable desire to draw others to God as well. We know of the love and goodness that comes from a relationship with Jesus Christ, the joy we feel in his presence, and we want those we love and care about to experience that same joy. We want to invite them to accompany us on our own journeys to deeper closeness with Jesus Christ.

But the truth is that many people either don't know how to invite others along or simply lack the conviction and the courage to do so. For some the word *evangelization* is so intimidating that it borders on impossible.

My hope is that this book will change that.

One way to accomplish this goal is by sharing my own experiences (both the successes and failures). I'll also share with you stories of others in this great big world who are stumbling toward perfection and trying to bring others along.

What I won't do is give you a concrete road map, a recipe book, or a conclusive "How to Be a Better Catholic in Thirty Days" guide. Instead, my goal is to give you a better understanding of why Catholicism is so awesome, help you incorporate it into your daily existence, and give you the confidence to encourage others to take daily steps closer to God.

chapter one
Who, Me?

> Don't panic.
>
> —Douglas Adams, *The Hitchhiker's Guide to the Galaxy*

As we begin to explore the possibilities of the New Evangelization, it could easily become overwhelming to imagine yourself being a part of it. There's something about the words *evangelization* and *evangelizing* that turns the stomachs of some people. Either they are intimidated by what others may think, afraid they'll come off like Bible thumpers, or just too lazy to go below the surface of what it means to be a Christian.

I want to reiterate here what I mentioned in the introduction (just in case you're like my wife and skipped it). My goal is to motivate you in three different areas:

1. to know (or *want* to know) your faith more deeply
2. to live your faith more fully
3. to share your faith more effectively.

All three things (knowing, living, and sharing) must be done in tandem, and all three are necessary for successful evangelization. For how could you share your faith if you don't know it very well? How could you live your faith without sharing it? How could you know your faith without living it?

The answer is, you can't.

I've had discussions with people who think they just can't do any more than they're already doing. They believe that they have gone as deep in their faith walk as is humanly possible (and they're probably right if they think growing in faith is an entirely human endeavor). They think they're old dogs who can't be taught new tricks. They're not convinced that God has a special place, plan, and purpose for them.

If you're one of those people, it's time to get over that. It's time to address your reservations head on, so you can become a New Evangelizer.

The Fear Factor

On October 22, 1978, six days after Karol Wojtyla's election as the first non-Italian pope in 455 years, the new pope spoke these words at his inaugural Mass:

> Brothers and sisters, do not be afraid to welcome Christ and accept his power. Help the Pope and all those who wish to serve Christ and with Christ's power to serve the human person and the whole of mankind. Do not be afraid. Open wide the doors for Christ. To his saving power open the boundaries of States, economic and political systems, the vast fields of culture, civilization and development. Do not be afraid.[1]

Throughout the next twenty-seven years, Pope John Paul II would repeat the words "Do not be afraid" time and again as he prepared the world for what he referred to as "the New Evangelization."

In the *Revised Standard Version* of the Bible, the phrase "Be not afraid" shows up six times. The phrase "Do not be afraid" can be found twenty-seven times. "Fear not" is in the Bible forty-three times, and the admonition "Have no fear" can be found eight times. The Bible has over three hundred passages about overcoming fear (see, for example, Deuteronomy 20:1; Joshua 1:9; 11:6; 2 Kings 1:15; Psalm 27:1–3; Luke 1:13, 30; 2:10).

Even Moses let his fear be known. He tried to offer excuses to God as to why he was a bad choice as prophet: "Oh, my Lord, I am not eloquent, either heretofore or since you have spoken to your servant; but I am slow of speech and of tongue" (Exodus 4:10).

God's answer to him? "Who has made man's mouth? Who makes him mute, or deaf, or seeing, or blind? Is it not I, the LORD? Now therefore go, and I will be with your mouth and teach you what you shall speak" (Exodus 4:11–12).

What's your excuse for not wanting to be a disciple in this world? Are you slow to speak? Do you have a hard time memorizing Scripture? Do you lose every argument you ever have? Are you too loud? Too quiet? Too boisterous? Too shy?

Maybe so. But where was God when those traits and behaviors showed themselves? Or rather, how much did you involve God in those moments?

In his book, *Crossing the Threshold of Hope*, Blessed John Paul II remembered the day back in 1978 when he proclaimed those words in St. Peter's Square. He wrote, "*Why should we have no fear? Because man has been redeemed by God…. The power of Christ's Cross and Resurrection is greater than any evil which man could or should fear.*"[2]

You may feel fear, but as God promised Moses, he "will be with your mouth and teach you what you shall speak."

New Evangelizers in Action: Bob McGivern and Greg Vens, Iowa Filmmakers

Bob McGivern and Greg Vens knew nothing about creating videos.

A Catholic from Davenport, Iowa, Bob is concerned about the boundaries that can divide Catholics. "I truly believe that many Catholics don't feel connected to others within their own parish, and they tend to overlook the vast community of faith," he says. "A good friend of mine left the Church not long ago to join a nondenominational Christian church where he found a community. This just frustrates me."

Wanting to build a sense of community at Our Lady of Lourdes parish in Bettendorf, Iowa, Bob contacted fellow parishioner Greg Vens about making some videos to show during Lent. "It wasn't clear to me what he wanted to do," Greg says. "But after talking over a few ideas, I got really excited. It was very motivating when we asked people to appear in the videos and saw how readily they agreed to help us out."

Several other parishioners became involved in producing the series. The videos weren't perfect, but it was evident that the Holy Spirit was at work.

"Many people told us how much they looked forward to the videos every week," Greg says. In fact, "people asked if we would be putting together another series." The next Lent they did just that.

Bob, Greg, and their colleagues learned a great deal about video technologies simply by going through the experience. Bob says, "This new social technology isn't going away, and if every diocese or parish would reach out this way, if there were more outreach tech-nology programs that sent communications (videos, talks, tweets, prayer e-mails) every day, then we as a faith community would be stronger. It would be awesome."

Links to the Lenten videos can be found at www.LourdesCatholic. com.

Who's Got Your Back?

I walked into the confessional at our local parish one summer Saturday afternoon back in 2002 and found the parochial vicar just sitting there, looking rather lonely. (It was the only scheduled opportunity for confession at our parish that week, and yet no one had shown up until then.) Father was praying over a single-decade knotted rosary made of black cord—thick, almost like the lace of a boot. On the end was a simple pewter crucifix.

"That's cool," I remember thinking. I took my place in the seat across from him and thought no more of that rosary.

A couple months later, just after Labor Day, I was sitting in the confines of the smallest cubicle in which I'd ever worked. To say it was small is somewhat of an understatement. At six-five and 250 pounds, I sat at my desk with one leg hanging out into the general walkway.

I was working on one random task or another when, for no reason other than perhaps the inspiration of the Holy Spirit, I recalled the single-decade rosary I'd seen in Fr. Michael's hands earlier in the summer.

Now, I don't particularly look like an arts-and-crafts kind of guy. To reiterate what I wrote above, I'm a rather big dude. Add to that the fact that I haven't had a hairline since 1995. I've never knitted, and I can't macramé (I'm not sure if anyone can anymore). But at that moment I had a compulsion beyond words. Honestly, it was almost as strong as when I decided I wanted to marry my wife and spend the rest of my life with her. In my mind, all I was thinking was, "I want to make one of those rosaries."

Even in 2002 I considered myself a fairly savvy purveyor of all things Google-able. So I opened a Web browser and typed "Knotted rosary instructions." I couldn't find much on how I'd even begin to make something like the rosary I'd seen that summer. I eventually discovered a website with basic instructions but without a single picture. I was clueless but still determined.

After work I drove straight to a large crafts store in search of nylon twine; I found nothing like what had been described in the instructions. I went to another store and struck out again. Eventually I bought the closest thing I could find: thin, ropelike material that only came in two colors, dark burgundy and black.

Strangely, or perhaps providentially, that same day I came upon a sign for a Catholic Church I'd never visited. I soon found myself inside, alone, staring at the tabernacle.

The visit to that church is significant for a few reasons. I didn't realize it at the time, but something life-changing was happening to me that day. I believe that just as she did throughout her life, our Blessed Mother Mary is constantly directing us to her Son, Jesus. She does this throughout Scripture, and she does this whenever we pray the rosary. She was doing that in my life that very day.

When we begin things in adoration and prayer, God can and will work through our fears, uncertainties, and insufficiencies to allow the Holy Spirit to do impossible things through us. For on that day an absolutely impossible thing began in me that has continued to magnify and grow for more than a decade now.

And it all started with being open to a small prompting from God.

Do you believe the Holy Spirit has your back?

> Say to those who are of a fearful heart:
> "Be strong, fear not!" (Isaiah 35:4)

A Different Kind of Army

After leaving the church I went home and sat on the floor and fought through the practically incoherent rosary-making instructions I'd found. I'd loop the cord around my finger three times, pull the twine through the middle, and somehow, like a magic trick, the knot I thought I was making simply disappeared. Presto!

I was about to give up, but I made yet one more attempt. I twisted the twine around my finger, pulled the end of the twine through the middle, and found myself staring at a perfect little knot. Then I made another, and another, and then I finished a decade, and I continued on.

That first rosary took me nearly two hours to figure out and complete. In the end it was an ugly, malformed, poorly spaced bundle of knots, but it was a rosary. And when it was completed, a sense of urgency came over me: I needed to make *more*.

This little thing I had just done, this weird little crafty thing, had meaning. I couldn't explain how or why, but I simply knew it did. And for someone who yearned to live for Christ, yet who also felt completely unprepared and unworthy to be one of his soldiers in the Church Militant of this world, that unexpected sense of purpose filled me with one of the greatest moments of peace I've ever experienced.

Not wanting to lose that elation, I grabbed another twenty-foot-long piece of twine and started another rosary. Within a week I'd made over twenty, and I started giving them to friends and family.

I found an out-of-state company that sold high-quality nylon twine in multiple colors. I started making rosaries upon request. I also gave them away to just about everyone I spoke to.

You have to understand something here. This isn't about me. It's about being open to what God might do through *you*. When it comes to knowing our faith, living our faith, and especially sharing our faith, we can't do it adequately on our own. But: "I can do all things in him who strengthens me" (Philippians 4:13).

God's timing could not have been any more perfect in my situation. I started making all-twine knotted rosaries in September 2002. The very next month Blessed Pope John Paul II declared the Year of the Rosary and introduced the luminous mysteries, the mysteries of light, to the world. How is it possible, if not for God, that I started making rosaries one month and the next month the pope declared the Year of the Rosary?

Several months and hundreds of all-twine knotted rosaries later, I was asked to give a talk at a youth group retreat about the power of the rosary. It was the first time I'd ever spoken on the topic, and I felt embarrassingly ill-prepared. Again I reminded myself of what God told Moses, "Now therefore go, and I will be with your mouth and teach you what you shall speak."

Perhaps you've had an experience like this: Completely unqualified, can't remember diddly-squat, suddenly presenting information far beyond your knowledge base or pay grade. But in faithfulness you turn it over to God and hear words coming out of your mouth that you are certain are not your own.

I told the teens that day how Jesus and Mary seemed to call me at just the right moment. I came to the realization, in the very middle of the talk, that if God called me to do this, he most likely was calling others to also take up their rosaries or to play some other vital role in the Church today. I made the comment, "It's not just about me making rosaries. But it's like I'm in an army for God."

After a short lesson in how to make the basic knots, the teens started making rosaries. Throughout the weekend they would come up to show me their finished rosaries. "Look," they'd say, "now I'm in the army too!"

That week our first apostolate, RosaryArmy.com, went online. In the years since, Rosary Army has been directly and indirectly responsible for the distribution of millions of rosaries. Rosary Army ended up being the very first Catholic organization to use podcasting technologies. In fact, we beat the Vatican to it by two weeks (though my wife always chides me when I brag about that).

Jennifer and I went on to create *That Catholic Show*, a video series used in parishes and homes around the world, found ourselves hosting a daily program on satellite radio, and eventually created an umbrella organization for all of our ministries, New Evangelizers. At NewEvangelizers.com we provide free resources to help people know their faith, live their faith, and share their faith in the New Evangelization. On that site, by the way, you can find rosary-making instructions we put together (with pictures), so you too can become a Rosary Army soldier.

Show up for Work, and Let God Lead the Way
If the Holy Spirit can manage to pull a diamond out of this six-foot-five chunk of coal, he can do it for everyone on this beautiful planet—everyone, that is, who is open to it.

Are you open? If not, pray that God will give you courage. Pray for God to remove your fear. Pray for the influx and influence of the Holy Spirit in your life.

If fear of the unknown or of doing something drastic for God paralyzes you, you're not the only one in history to feel that way. Toss that fear aside.

"Here I am," the young Samuel said. "Speak, for your servant hears" (1 Samuel 3:4, 10).

God might have plans for you, small or large, that you could never imagine. I've seen it time and again in my own life that, when I'm open to God leading me, when I allow the Holy Spirit to work through me, miraculous and amazing things happen. And the Holy Spirit wants to do the same for you.

God is calling. Are you ready to listen? Are you ready for action?

Questions

1. Do you feel any amount of fear (small or large) at the idea of talking about Jesus to others?

2. Has there been a time when you tried to talk about God to someone, and the situation made you feel as if you weren't smart or knowledgeable enough for the conversation?

3. What are some concrete steps you could take to strengthen the areas of weakness in your faith life? What might help you overcome your fears?

Prayer for Courage

Lord,

please give me courage to love you.

Give me courage to serve you.

Give me courage to tell others about you.

Give me courage to grow closer to you.

Give me courage to live my life as you call me to.

Give me courage to pick up my cross each day as you
   picked up yours.

Remove from me all fear,

so that you can put me to work for your kingdom.

Amen.

chapter two
Defining the New Evangelization

> It always seems impossible until it's done.
> —Nelson Mandela[1]

Blessed Pope John Paul II first used the term "New Evangelization" in a homily during his historic visit to Poland in June 1979. "A *new evangelization* has begun," he said, "as if it were a new proclamation, even if in reality it is the same as ever."[2]

That's an important thing to remember from the beginning: When we discuss the *New* Evangelization, it does not mean spreading a new message. The message that is being spread is the exact message of salvation that has been preached for two thousand years. It is the message that "God sent forth his Son, born of a woman, born under the law, to redeem those who were under the law, so that we might receive adoption as sons" (Galatians 4:4–5). It is the message of "the gospel of Jesus Christ, the Son of God" (Mark 1:1).

In our faith we have the greatest message the world has ever known or ever will receive. We may not yet know that message as well as we should, but our ignorance (willful or accidental) does not negate the truth of the message that has been shared from generation to generation.

What is *new* in the New Evangelization? What have changed are the various *methods of delivering* the message and the need to proclaim it to a society that has largely forgotten or ignored it.

A Clear Definition

If you were to ask ten people to explain what the New Evangelization is, you'd most likely get ten different answers. And theoretically, all ten answers could be correct.

"New media is New Evangelization," one might say, "blogs, podcasts, social networking. All of that. That's New Evangelization."

That answer is only partially correct. Yes, new media can help you to better know your faith. Blogs and podcasts and so on can educate and catechize you in the spiritual, historical, biblical, and other foundational aspects of the Catholic faith. And creators of new media have a great way of being witnesses to the modern world. But "new media" is not the message. New media is just one delivery method out of many. Books, television, and radio (which some would consider "traditional" or "old" media) play roles just as important as new media.

Another person could say, "New Evangelization is working in my home and in my parish to help everyone—including myself—to better understand their faith."

This too would be correct, but it would only encompass a fraction of what the New Evangelization is. A part of the New Evangelization does consist in developing a more sacramentally rich faith, for the graces we receive in the sacraments allow us to live the life of the Spirit more fully. There are many other specific examples of New Evangelization in action.

"New Evangelization" was a recurring theme in the various encyclicals and letters of Blessed John Paul II's pontificate. Through these statements we can get a more vibrant and clear image of what New Evangelization is.

> [R]evealed truth beckons reason—God's gift fashioned for the assimilation of truth—to enter into its light and thereby come to understand in a certain measure what it has believed.[3]

> The witness of a Christian life is the first and irreplaceable form of mission: Christ, whose mission we continue, is the "witness" *par excellence* (Revelation 1:5; 3:14) and the model of all Christian witness. The Holy Spirit accompanies the Church along her way and associates her with the witness he gives to Christ (see John 15:26–27).[4]

> In the complex reality of mission, initial proclamation has a central and irreplaceable role.... Faith is born of preaching, and every ecclesial community draws its origin and life from the personal response of each believer to that preaching.[5]

In essence, New Evangelization is comprised of three things: First, New Evangelization includes renewed spiritual devotion as well as renewed efforts in catechesis. We must know Jesus, and we must understand Christianity and the Catholic faith in particular. This renewed knowledge enables the second element, living our faith. And third, a natural extension of knowing and living our faith is to share it with others.

The challenge, one that both Blessed John Paul II and Pope Benedict XVI have given to each of us, is to learn how to renew the hearts, minds, and lives of Christians and non-Christians alike in a definitively secular landscape. This is the task of the New Evangelization.

New Evangelizers in Action: Gabriel Doman, a "Radioactive Catholic"

"Although I am a cradle Catholic, I grew up in what my pastor calls 'the felt-and-burlap period,'" says Gabriel Doman of the diocese of Columbus, Ohio. "Catechesis meant making a felt-and-burlap banner that said, 'God Is Love,' and that basically covered it."

Like many people born in the 1960s and 1970s, Gabriel found himself well into his twenties before he first heard many foundational Catholic terms like *transubstantiation*. "When I joined the Knights of Columbus in 1999, at the age of thirty-four," Gabriel says, "I did not know how to pray the rosary."

Now, years later, Gabriel is financial secretary for his Knights of Columbus council, is active in the Apostolate for Family Consecration, and occasionally tweets and retweets information related to family consecration. He also makes an effort to attend the Columbus Catholic Men's Conference each year.

What made the difference?

"I have learned more about Catholicism the past three years, listening to Catholic radio and reading books featured on Catholic radio, than I had learned in the previous forty-four years," says Gabriel. "In my younger days I certainly wanted to know my faith better. I just did not know where to start."

When looking at the future of the Church, Gabriel says, "I have great hope in the New Evangelization and am very impressed by the younger generation. I have had several opportunities to interact with Catholics in their twenties recently, and they are much better prepared to face the temptations of the world and live out their faith than my generation was. The Millennials will set the world on fire for the faith."

Disciples Called to Witness

In 2012 the United States Conference of Catholic Bishops Committee on Evangelization and Catechesis released a document called *Disciples Called to Witness: The New Evangelization.* This document highlights five primary points of the New Evangelization: the current cultural context, the historical context, the focus of the New Evangelization itself, its culture, and the key components of outreach programs specifically recommended for the New Evangelization.

In many ways the document is like a mini Bible and *Catechism* study, thanks to the multiple Scripture and Church document references provided throughout. The result is a veritable road map of information regarding past and present evangelization efforts within the Catholic Church. At its core, as with many other Church documents focusing on evangelization, is the fact that each of us as Christians is called to proclaim the gospel, the Good News, to all people everywhere and at all times.

Acts 1:8 says, "You shall receive power when the Holy Spirit has come upon you, and you shall be my witnesses...to the end of the earth." This was the directive Jesus gave his disciples, and it is also at the core of modern efforts at evangelization. The disciples were given the task of the original, primary evangelization: letting the entire world know of the existence of Jesus Christ, King of Kings, Lord of Lords, and our Savior and Messiah. The goal of the modern Church is the same: "The New Evangelization seeks to invite modern man and culture into a relationship with Jesus Christ and his Church."[6]

The original evangelization was for a world that had never encountered Jesus Christ; the secondary, New Evangelization is, in part, for those John Paul II recognized as "the baptized [who] have lost a living sense of the faith, or even no longer consider themselves members of the Church, and live a life far removed from Christ and his Gospel."[7]

It's hard to imagine anyone in this world who has not heard of Jesus Christ. For those who have still not been introduced to the Savior, the original evangelization remains. And for our modern world and culture, where "Jesus Christ" is often used more as a swear word than as the name of our God and Creator, a secondary evangelization is in order. For both we draw inspiration and encouragement from the Gospel and the rest of the New Testament in engaging those around us, and ourselves, in a renewed relationship with Jesus Christ our Redeemer and his Church.

Staring up at the Clouds

Some people (perhaps you're one of them) read the missionary directive of Acts 1:8 and don't necessarily apply it to their own lives. "Great Scripture! Very moving! So glad we have people [not me!] to do this heavy work!" But the fact is that Jesus gave the apostles a command that applies to us to this very day: "You shall be my witnesses in Jerusalem and in all Judea and Samaria and to the end of the earth."

How often do you and I, in our attempts to live out our Catholic faith, fail to realize that we are called to be witnesses in this world?

Do we realize that admonition to proclaim the gospel to the world still applies to us today?

We may think, "In my family, at home, I can be a witness; that's good enough." Or we may say, "I can have my own personal relationship with Jesus Christ, and that's all I need." The Catholic Church teaches us otherwise.

If you are baptized, if you've been confirmed, and indeed every time you receive the Blessed Sacrament in Holy Communion, God gives you the graces you need to be his disciple and live out that challenge, that clarion call of Jesus Christ.

Were the disciples afraid from time to time? I imagine so. They were human, after all. Even after Jesus ascended into heaven before their very eyes, they stood around, staring blankly into the sky, doing nothing until two angels of God appeared to push them on their way (see Acts 1:10–11).

We sometimes have to stop and ask ourselves if we are disciples, or if we are just standing around looking up at the sky, waiting for Jesus to come back to transform the world. Our call is to do what the disciples did: turn around, get moving, engage those we encounter, love them, and encourage them to experience Jesus's love and mercy through the Church.

Honestly, it can be painful to be a Christian in today's culture. It's easy to go to church and to have prayer time and study time (though we may struggle from time to time to have those things). But the challenge of going out and witnessing to others and being open to the Holy Spirit in potentially uncomfortable and uncertain circumstances is another matter.

Yet there are millions of people in this world who are hungry for the mercy and forgiveness of our Lord. There are many who once knew God's love but no longer actively seek it or even believe themselves worthy of it. It is in God's mercy and forgiveness that we experience true comfort. Don't we want that same comfort for everyone we encounter? If we are to be disciples, tasked with the challenge of going out and being witnesses to the ends of the earth, we must keep in mind that mercy and forgiveness of God.

How many people do we know who are fractured inside and separated from God? How many of our relatives have walked away from the Church for one reason or another? Have we invited them back to be reconciled, so that they too can partake of the Eucharist, the grace-filled meal?

What Am I Going to Do?

The problem with the phrase "New Evangelization" is that some people tend to think, "Well, if it's so new, I'm going to wait to see if it catches on." Sort of like New Coke. Not everything new works.

The temptation is to wait and see what others are going to do. "I wonder what my priest is going to do with this." Or, "I'm going to wait and see what the bishop is going to do." But the question you need to ask is, "What am I going to do?" The New Evangelization has a role for every one of us to play, and it is imperative—downright mandatory—that we all play our roles in this effort.

Evangelization is not new. Evangelization has been around since the time of Christ. What's new in the New Evangelization is the focus of our efforts.

In the mid-1970s Pope Paul VI wrote a letter called *Evangelii Nuntiandi* about preaching the gospel and sharing the Catholic faith in today's world. This document, along with the documents that came out of Vatican II, provide a framework for presenting Catholicism to a modern audience. In effect, the work of Pope Paul VI established a foundation for the New Evangelization work of his successors.

During the thirty-plus years of Pope John Paul II's pontificate that followed, the *Catechism of the Catholic Church*, *Redemptoris Missio* (On the Permanent Validity of the Church's Missionary Mandate), and other documents were akin to gathering the kindling for a major bonfire. With every document, with every journey, with every canonization, with every proclamation of "Be not afraid!" John Paul II carefully, methodically, and regularly added more wood to the fire.

In addition to the term *New Evangelization*, Blessed John Paul II also regularly used the word *springtime* to describe what God is doing in the Church. In his 1990 *Redemptoris Missio*, for example, he wrote: "As the third millennium of the redemption draws near, God is preparing a great springtime for Christianity, and we can already see its first signs."[8]

After three decades of fuel-gathering, Pope Benedict XVI ascended to the papacy. He released messages about Christian hope (*Spe Salvi*), Christian love (*Deus Caritas Est*), and more. In 2011 he instituted the Pontifical Council for the New Evangelization and declared a Year of Faith from October 2012 to November 2013, with a special focus on the New Evangelization. With these events Pope Benedict lit the match and bent forward to set the pile on fire through the Holy Spirit, who enkindles us all with his love.

In other words, the New Evangelization, though building for several decades, is just now catching fire. And when that fire is finally set alight, imagine the light that the world will witness through those who are ready to fan those flames.

We are still in the springtime of which Pope John Paul II spoke, and most likely we will be for some time, in the same way that the Catholic Church has been in the "end times" since the passion of our Lord Jesus Christ.

Three out of Three

When I worked full-time in the information technology industry, there was an adage we frequently used when tackling a software or Web development project: You can get the product you want, but you'll have to settle for just two of the three conditions you're asking for.

When a customer would approach us with a project requirement, it was not uncommon for there to be some level of priority associated with the proposed work. The customer usually wanted the work done quickly. In most cases the customer would also expect the project to look good, work as intended, and be easy to use. Lastly, it was not uncommon for a customer to also want the best deal. So in most situations the customer would want the work done quickly, well, and inexpensively.

The problem is that, in the business world, it is virtually impossible to get all three of those things. You can get a well-built product quickly, but it'll cost you, because the best and highest paid people will have to be brought in for the job. Or a project can be done quickly and inexpensively, but the final result probably won't be what you're looking for. Or, you can get something cheap and well-built, but the project might take longer: The entry-level people on the low end of the pay scale may not finish it as expeditiously as seasoned workers would.

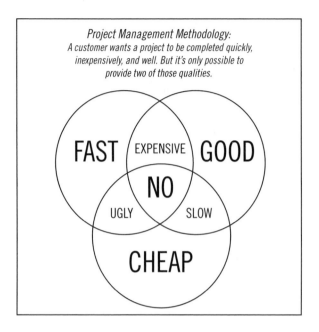

Project Management Methodology:
A customer wants a project to be completed quickly,
inexpensively, and well. But it's only possible to
provide two of those qualities.

FAST EXPENSIVE GOOD

NO

UGLY SLOW

CHEAP

When it comes to the New Evangelization, again we have three components: know the faith, live the faith, and share the faith. But unlike the business world, the New Evangelization must have all three aspects at once.

Many people love the idea of what Jesus has to offer (salvation and the joy of heaven) but aren't willing to give all of what it takes to receive that. They want to give their faith one or two aspects of their lives but not their entire lives.

In 2011, at the conclusion of the first plenary assembly of the recently formed Pontifical Council for the New Evangelization, Pope Benedict XVI addressed the fact that many people in the Church today have a viewpoint that is more in line with the secular culture than with the Church.

> [W]e are witnessing a drama of fragmentation which no
> longer acknowledges a unifying reference point; more-
> over, it often occurs that people wish to belong to the
> Church, but they are strongly shaped by a vision of life
> which is in contrast with the faith.[9]

Perhaps people call themselves Catholic yet support abortion. Or
they subscribe to the Catholic label yet use contraception. They
always fill in "Catholic" on forms that ask for religious preference
but do little to show care for the poor.

The reason for this anomaly, the Holy Father suggested, is that
people have excluded God from their lives. They've adopted the
attitudes and lifestyles of the world, perhaps without even realizing it. They stick to the Catholic label but fail to actually give
their lives to Christ in a complete and meaningful way. They
attend church but don't allow God to transform them in tangible
ways.

If you have a scholarly and well-read understanding of
Catholicism, and you gladly share that knowledge with others,
but you're not actually living out the teachings of the faith, then
you're a hypocrite. Similarly, if you know the faith and actually
live it by never missing Mass, by regularly going to confession,
and by spending great amounts of time in prayer and study, but
you never actively share the faith with others, then the only one
who is benefitting is you. Again, you're not fully embracing your
Catholic faith.

And lastly, if you're living the faith by being active at church
and sharing the faith by serving others, but you don't take the
time to truly know Jesus and the teachings of the faith, you may
be leading others astray without even realizing it.

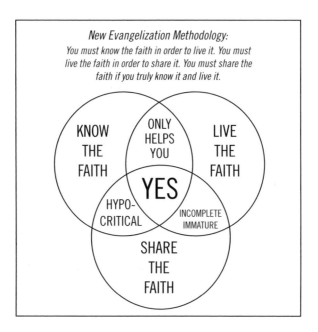

The New Evangelization is a re-introduction of Jesus Christ to the world. It starts with us. We must constantly strive to include all three aspects of the New Evangelization in our daily lives.

This may seem overwhelming—perhaps you've tried and failed in the past—but the good news is that there are ways to make the New Evangelization a success in your own life as well as in the lives of others. And I'm going to show you how.

Questions

1. Knowing there are multiple aspects of New Evangelization, how would you describe New Evangelization to someone else?

2. Is there an area of evangelization in which you think God may be calling you?

Prayer for Grace

Lord, please give me more grace,
strengthen my faith,
and increase my knowledge of you and your Church,
so that I will be full of faith and full of joy
in my proclamation and witness of Jesus Christ to those
around me.
Amen.

chapter three
Don't Be Squishy

> Increase our faith!
> —LUKE 17:5

"Every believer is called to the challenge of the new evangelization." That's one of the most telling statements of Pope Benedict XVI, addressed to a group of newly appointed bishops in October 2012. The pope went on to say that bishops must "boldly invite the people from every walk of life to an encounter with Christ and to render more solid the faith."[1]

You might be thinking, "Well, that sounds all well and good, I suppose. But I don't think that really applies to me. There's nothing that I have to do, is there?"

Well, if you thought you'd escape from doing something in the New Evangelization, I'm sorry to inform you, my friend, that you're out of luck.

Both of these statements are vitally important, and they tie together, though they're addressing two different audiences. The first audience includes the everyday layperson, that is, you and me. If you believe in God, if you've been baptized, then you're one of the members of the "every believer" crowd. The pope has personally challenged *you*. You have to get off your lazy laurels and do something.

Now the question is: What are you going to do?

Personal Renewal

Keep in mind that the heart of the New Evangelization is re-introducing Jesus Christ and the Catholic faith, specifically in the areas of the world where Christianity was previously present, thriving, and respected. The New Evangelization, according to Cardinal Timothy Dolan, is "the rekindling of faith in persons and cultures where it has grown lackluster."[2]

The *Instrumentum Laboris* document used to plan the 2012 Synod of Bishops identifies the New Evangelization as "an adequate response to the signs of the times, to the needs of individuals...and to the new sectors" of the world, "with their cultures through which we express our identity and the meaning of our lives."[3] In other words, we need to discover how to reach people in this world of rapidly evolving cultures and sociological differences. These people are searching for greater purpose and place in their families and communities. Are they finding guidance and direction from a relationship with Jesus Christ and the Catholic Church?

In many cases they're not. So what can we do to show them that Jesus can bring more meaning to their lives? How can we introduce them to Jesus and help them have a relationship with him?

Again, this is something that must begin within us. "The New Evangelization generates enthusiastic missionaries; those in the apostolate of the mission *ad gentes* [the missionary activity of the Church] require themselves to be constantly evangelized anew."[4]

This is good news for each of us. In the New Evangelization we have opportunities to strengthen our faith!

Do you need a moment of grace, a deeper experience of the strengthening love of God? Do you want to draw closer to him?

We all do. We all need grace and that increase of love.

An important part of the New Evangelization is knowing our faith more fully. So how would you answer these basic questions?

- Who is Jesus Christ?
- Why should I develop a relationship with him?
- How do I best know him, love him, and serve him?
- And what is Catholicism anyway?

In chapter ten I give you some ideas for how to "grow" your own faith. But remember that God is the one who draws you to himself. The conundrum of how to approach and understand every aspect of the New Evangelization, in fact, becomes somewhat easier when we look at it in this light: It's not just our problem; it's God's problem.

Without his help we can do nothing, but "I can do all things in him who strengthens me" (Philippians 4:13).

So while you have a responsibility to show up for the job, to continue to develop your spirituality, and to grow closer to God, you can make a good part of this God's problem. Ask him for grace.

"So you, my child, be strong in the grace that is in Christ Jesus" (2 Timothy 2:1). The grace doesn't come from you. It doesn't come from within. You can't just snap your fingers and conjure up grace. That's not how it works. Grace is a gift. And grace is what is needed to grow in your relationship with Jesus Christ and to be an effective evangelizer.

New Evangelizers in Action: Fr. Charles Zlock—Pushing Forward

When asked what the biggest challenge is in living out his faith as a Catholic priest, Fr. Charles Zlock, a priest in the archdiocese of Philadelphia, says, "An almost hostile, in-your-face, belligerent 'I will not follow and I will not participate' attitude against the faith from fallen-away Catholics."

That's a struggle for many people who dedicate their lives to Christ in a world that wants to ignore him. But Fr. Zlock pushes forward, trying to reach the world where it is. He leads conferences at the local Malvern Retreat House and is active on his website, blog, Twitter, and Facebook. Father constantly seeks to develop his own knowledge of the faith, sometimes encountering an ironic obstacle.

"Deciding from the richness of our faith and the significant amount of new material coming out in various new media formats is one of the biggest challenges," he says. "Which books and sources should I focus on to feed my faith more effectively and pass … on to others?"

Fr. Zlock is optimistic for the New Evangelization. "I hope for a new outpouring of the Holy Spirit, much like we saw after Vatican II," he says. That outpouring, he says, has led to other "exciting new laity-led initiatives, like Kings Men, Fatherhood and Leadership Institute, Theology of the Body Institute, and more."

You can follow Fr. Zlock's continuing efforts in the New Evangelization at www.FrZlock.com.

Measure for Measure

When you take on a task—whether it be a term paper, a house renovation, a project at work, losing weight, or potty-training a kid—it's typical to set some sort of parameters to determine, at the end, whether you've been successful or not. It's necessary to set some goals to measure how well you've done on any given challenge.

If you finish your term paper on time and get a good grade, you were successful.

If the new room in your house is completed and on budget, you were successful.

If your team reaches all its requirements for the quarter, you were successful.

If you lose twenty pounds, you were successful.

And if your son can make it to the toilet without relieving himself on the floor, you were successful.

So how will you know a year from now, a month from now, or a week from now that you are making any measurable progress in your faith development?

Granted, it's a lot more difficult to measure spiritual goals than many other goals in life. How do you know when your faith is better? And once you reach your "faith goal," then what?

While you can't necessarily create a goal such as, "I want to increase my grace level by 20 percent," you can set realistic spiritual goals, such as, "I want to spend at least one hour a month in Eucharistic Adoration." Writing such goals down and keeping track of how faithful you are to them can be hugely beneficial to your spiritual development.

Think about the way most people address the Lenten season each year. In late winter, as Ash Wednesday approaches, Christians find themselves faced with the annual question, "What am I giving up for Lent?" Now, in recent years I've found it beneficial to not only choose something to do without but also to choose at least one additional spiritual practice to more firmly develop my faith. Usually I try to increase my prayer, study, fasting, and almsgiving.

One year I made a commitment to read St. Paul's Letter to the Romans as many times as possible, with a minimum of two concentrated readings during the Lenten season. (I was trying to set a realistic goal, aiming for success and encouragement rather than failure and frustration.) Reading this specific book of the Bible multiple times wasn't necessarily giving something up (unless you count the time I gave up for that extra spiritual reading); rather it added to my regular routine.

Now, years later, I still regularly recall many parts of Romans that I spent extra time pondering during Lent. Reading this book really helped me grow in my relationship with the Lord, particularly in the area of trusting him. "We know that in everything God works for good with those who love him, who are called according to his purpose" (Romans 8:28).

Identifying and adopting specific spiritual practices does not need to be saved for the Lenten season. We can put goals in place as needed throughout the year. Every day presents opportunities to deepen our faith. "Behold, now is the acceptable time; behold, now is the day of salvation" (2 Corinthians 6:2).

The Bishops' Role

Let's go back to the statement Pope Benedict XVI made specifically to bishops: "Boldly invite the people from every walk of life to an encounter with Christ and to render more solid the faith."[5]

Your Excellencies who might have come across this book, I, as one of the lay faithful, ask you to please listen to this admonition of the Holy Father. He did not just say that bishops must invite people to an encounter with Christ; he said that you must do so *boldly*.

The pope's phrase "Render more solid the faith" should be our anthem of daily living. We don't want a squishy kind of faith. Faith cannot be like a big wad of Play-Doh. What happens when you squeeze a ball of Play-Doh in your hands? It comes gooshing out from between your fingers, falls away, dries up, hardens, and becomes useless. It becomes disposable.

In today's world there are far too many people who treat Catholicism like a squishy ball of Play-Doh. This lackluster attitude and oftentimes outright disdain for Catholicism has at its root a terrible malady called secularism. Pope Benedict XVI warns that "secularization, which presents itself in cultures by imposing a world and humanity without reference to Transcendence, is invading every aspect of daily life and developing a mentality in which God is effectively absent, wholly or partially, from human life and awareness."[6]

This idea of life without transcendence—without an encounter with the Father, Son, and Holy Spirit—is something that should make us incredibly sad. We live in a world where cultures and lifestyles contrary to moral and natural law, let alone the teachings of the Catholic Church, are glaringly the norm. These minimize the importance and legitimacy of faith in modern society. We witness attacks on religious liberty, on marriage, on children, on women, on the unborn, and on the elderly. Forgotten are God's loving care and his perspective on the dignity of humanity.

How many people do you know who at one point held a deep love and conviction for God and the Church but, maybe a little bit at a time, fell away from not only Catholicism but an ongoing relationship with God? Even more troubling than secularization's chipping away at individual souls is its markedly negative impact on the Church. As Pope Benedict pointed out, "This secularization is not only an external threat to believers, but has been manifest for some time in the heart of the Church herself."[7]

But if faith is *firm*, if it's solid like the rock upon which Jesus Christ established the Catholic Church, nothing can overcome it. Our faith is a hearty faith, and when we take the time to learn about and understand it, it becomes a clear faith that applies to every aspect of our lives.

When we have shepherds who *boldly* invite us to an encounter with Jesus Christ, this is the kind of faith each and every member of the Church and every Christian in the world is capable of possessing. When we have shepherds who *boldly* instruct their flocks to become more effective witnesses, entire families and communities can be transformed into modern-day versions of the ancient Church, where shepherds and their flocks lived as committed disciples of Jesus Christ and were eager to witness to the world the Good News of the salvation he offers.

The faith needs credible witnesses. I like the term *credible*. The bishops, as the first witnesses of the faith, can only serve people if they first are at the service of God.

There are unfortunately many non-credible witnesses of Catholicism in the world today. We see politicians who support abortion during the week and then receive the Eucharist on Sunday. We know there are Catholics who fill the pews at Mass but contracept in the bedroom. The world is full of people who say, "I'm Catholic," when it's time to take a survey, but when it comes to regular Mass attendance or living a life of chastity (not to be confused with living a life of celibacy), they're nowhere to be seen.

We need to be *credible* witnesses, willing to carry the crosses and burdens of our faith that often make it difficult to be Catholic. We must embrace the sometimes difficult tenets of the Church.

Sometimes I think it would be a heck of a lot easier *not* to be Catholic! It would be a lot easier to just do what *I* want in this world rather than try to follow Christ. It wouldn't be better for my eternal soul, of course. It wouldn't do any good for the people around me either, as that kind of attitude and behavior will never draw anyone to Jesus.

So I want to be an ever more credible witness, acknowledging my weaknesses and shortcomings and areas in need of improvement, pressing on to live my life fully devoted to Christ and the gospel. I want to be firm in the faith rather than molded by a secularized world.

We need shepherds who are willing to boldly lead in this area. And lay Catholics need to be ready and willing to obey our shepherds, as the Letter to the Hebrews tells us: "Remember your leaders, those who spoke to you the word of God; consider the outcome of their life, and imitate their faith.... Do not be led away by diverse and strange teachings" (Hebrews 13:7, 9).

It's Not All Relative

At a recent Mass an older priest said something during his homily that somewhat took me by surprise. It surprised me not because it was wrong but because it was so right. Sad to say, I have gotten used to priests his age who are not willing to say anything about difficult Church teachings—you know, those truths that some members of a secularly influenced congregation may not readily welcome.

This priest said that for many people in the modern Catholic Church, since Vatican II, the problem is not the lack of theology but the lack of respect for liturgy: lack of respect for the Mass, lack of respect for Jesus Christ in the Eucharist, lack of respect for the sacrament of marriage, lack of respect for the celebration of all these things and more.

This priest's ordination was conferred in the shadow of Vatican II. U.S. culture was changing with the rise of the sexual revolution and other sorts of pandemonium. Many sincere but misguided people in the Church were delving into what some in my generation refer to as "Kumbaya Catholicism." This period marked the onset of holding hands during the Our Father, liturgical dancing with colorful ribbons, and puppetry and clown acts during the Liturgy of the Word and even the Liturgy of the Eucharist.

I point this out not as some sort of attack on the good men and other religious who have devoted their lives in service to the Church. Neither do I wish to denigrate those who engaged in liturgical practices for which there were no rubrics. Rather I want to highlight the fact that the Catholicism to which I was introduced in my youth was often a Catholicism formed more by the emotional resonance of the times than by the truth and beauty that comes to us through the teaching authority of the Church. I lived in multiple cities and states and attended a variety of Catholic parishes. I feel I was short-changed in many ways in my catechesis and instruction in the faith.

Thankfully, God can take misguided enthusiasm that led to potentially abusive liturgical practices and redirect the Church to where he originally intended, a truly Holy Spirit–inspired place of worship that is rich in sacraments and the celebration of the faith. Additionally, he can take those of us who may not have the best Catholic education—perhaps that education stopped after our confirmation, around the age of fifteen or even younger—and use even our limited knowledge as a springboard for doing amazing things for the Church and the world.

Every Catholic's journey toward living in obedience to the fullness of the faith is different. The beauty is that our destination (or our target destination, at least) is the same. We want to get to heaven.

Let me be clear here. When I say that people's journeys may vary, I'm specifically referring to the individual journeys people take as they grow in a greater understanding of our Catholic faith here on this earth. I am not talking about different ways of getting to heaven. The way to heaven is simple to define but often challenging to live. A most basic set of steps includes accepting Jesus Christ as Savior, repenting of sins, and striving to live righteously so as not to lose the redemption freely offered.

Some people suggest that there is some wiggle room about how we are allowed to live. "As long as I'm a good person, I'm OK and will get to heaven," one might say. Another person might justify his behavior by saying, "I don't believe that a loving God would send me to hell just because I'm living with my girlfriend." Now, that would be correct. God won't send him to hell. But that man's choice to live in a way that separates him from God would send him to hell.

A sneakier approach I've encountered revolves around the statement "One goal with many paths." The underlying intention here is that no one should be concerned with how someone else chooses to live and that we'll all eventually get to heaven. The idea is that we don't need a set path, road map, or religion to make that happen. Again, if you're a good person, you'll get to heaven.

But that's not necessarily true. The idea betrays a sensibility that is rife with relativism, which is the erroneous philosophy that what is true for you may not be true for me, but that both truths can somehow coexist. For example, if one person was to say the sky is blue, and another person says the sky is yellow, a relativist would suggest that if those answers make a person happy, and if each person believes his answer to be true, then both answers are allowable. I hope you can see the ridiculousness of this viewpoint.

Let's take this notion to a more frequent scenario. Look at the Catholic Church teaching, based on Scriptures such as John 6 (the Bread of Life Discourse), that Jesus Christ becomes physically present in the Eucharist. A Protestant or someone of another faith background would suggest that John 6 is only symbolic, not to be taken literally. A relativist would say that both beliefs can somehow be true, though they contradict each other completely.

On April 18, 2005, the day before he was elected pope, Cardinal Joseph Ratzinger, then the dean of the College of Cardinals, preached at the Mass for the Election of the Supreme Pontiff at St. Peter's Basilica. During that homily, the soon-to-be-named pope acknowledged the reality of the difficulties in having a concise faith that adheres closely to the teachings of the Catholic Church:

> Today, having a clear faith based on the Creed of the
> Church is often labeled as fundamentalism. Whereas

relativism, that is, letting oneself be "tossed here and there, carried about by every wind of doctrine," seems the only attitude that can cope with modern times. We are building a dictatorship of relativism that does not recognize anything as definitive and whose ultimate goal consists solely of one's own ego and desires.[8]

Catholicism recognizes something *very definitive*: a faith based on the Creed of the Church, which offers a well-defined pathway for living. That pathway is often narrow, and it includes many challenges. But the challenges are not nearly as perilous as the morally relativistic offerings of today's secular society.

> Enter by the narrow gate; for the gate is wide and the way is easy, that leads to destruction, and those who enter by it are many. For the gate is narrow and the way is hard, that leads to life, and those who find it are few. (Matthew 7:13–14)

The truth is that God wants us to be with him in heaven, and he's clear on what it takes to get there. God has entrusted to the Catholic Church the fullness of the faith, with the wisdom on how to reach our ultimate goal. To suggest that the Church's teachings— and by logical extension, God's teachings—are nothing more than optional suggestions and that more convenient lifestyles are acceptable to God is at best naive and at worst willfully ignorant and potentially sinful.

In other words, truth is truth. And to pretend otherwise is what has gotten our world into the state in which we now find it, awash in relativism and contradictory truths.

Questions

1. Have there been moments in your life when, talking with others, you found it difficult to be honest in admitting your feelings for and relationship with Jesus Christ?
2. What is one area in which you'd like to have a better understanding of your faith a week from now? What about a month or year from now?
3. How could you be a more credible witness to the faith in the world today?

Prayer for Internal Change

Lord,

my ultimate desire is to know you and serve you in this world

so as to spend eternity with you in the next.

Sometimes my own beliefs, opinions, and desires get in the way of knowing your will.

Please send your Holy Spirit to conform my will to yours, especially in the areas where I am the most resistant.

Please give me the strength to be a witness to others who might also struggle in living for you.

Amen.

chapter four
Deserts and Dark Nights

> Have I not commanded you? Be strong and of good
> courage; be not frightened, neither be dismayed; for
> the LORD your God is with you wherever you go.
> —JOSHUA 1:9

Far from being something new and innovative, the call for a
better modern-day understanding and practice of evangelization
can be traced back several years. In June 1973, Pope Paul VI, in
an address to the College of Cardinals, stated, "The conditions
of the society in which we live oblige all of us therefore to revise
methods, to seek by every means to study how we can bring the
Christian message to modern man. For it is only in the Christian
message that modern man can find the answer to his questions
and the energy for his commitment of human solidarity."[1]

There is no doubt that proclaiming the gospel in today's world
is a difficult challenge. Though the Christian message is vital
to modern man, many people stray down blind alleys—online
communities, the accumulation of Facebook friends, drugs, sex,
politics—to fulfill their inner longings and to escape the cloud of
fear and discouragement and anxiety that hovers over them.

The National Health and Nutritional Examination Survey, conducted by the Centers for Disease Control, reports that one in ten people over age twelve in the United States is taking an antidepressant.[2] While many people have a legitimate need for prescription help in dealing with various mental illnesses, there might be something causing an elevated need for pharmaceutical intervention. There definitely seems to be a high level of desire among people to find contentment and happiness.

To all who are willing to accept it, the gospel—the Good News of the salvation offered by Jesus Christ—is the answer, "the way, and the truth, and the life" (John 14:6). I hope you count yourself among those numbers.

We look to the Church for encouragement and to the sacraments for the strength and grace to live out our baptismal call to evangelize, to be disciples in this world. And through that God-given grace, we may experience the joy of Jesus Christ, his ever-enduring love, and the excitement of not only knowing and living out our faith but also desiring to share it with the world. This is at the core of evangelization.

It is important to highlight here the fact that we're not talking about revising the message; we're talking about new delivery efforts. Catholicism has the greatest message the world has ever known: "God so loved the world that he gave his only-begotten Son, that whoever believes in him should not perish but have eternal life" (John 3:16). Despite the simplicity of that message, far too many people aren't checking their inboxes to receive it.

Let's Get out of the Desert
In one of his first homilies as Holy Father, Pope Benedict XVI said, "The Church as a whole and all her Pastors, like Christ,

must set out to lead people out of the desert, towards the place of life, towards friendship with the Son of God, towards the One who gives us life, and life in abundance."[3]

How can we, the Church, "lead people out of the desert"?

The initial goal for all of us—pastors and laity alike—is pretty clear: Get out of the desert ourselves! Get out of the dryness of a routine faith, of going through the motions out of obligation!

If you remain stagnant in your faith, you'll wither and die. Instead of sticking around in the sand dunes, dive into the ocean of faith. There is something new to discover each day. The more you live the faith, the deeper will be your desire to grow closer to God. And as you learn to share the faith, you will know the satisfaction of witnessing the Holy Spirit working through *you* in reaching others.

If you don't get anything out of Mass, what are you putting into it?

If you find the Catholic faith boring, when was the last time you read a book explaining the Eucharist or narrating the life of a saint?

If you don't feel the presence of God, perhaps you need to spend more time with him in prayer.

If you think that the struggle of learning about and living your faith isn't worth it, then perhaps you've never opened yourself to the joy that comes through suffering.

Jesus Christ found himself in a desert for forty days. In the midst of those forty days, he turned to prayer and fasting. He fought temptation with the Word of God. The devil was no match against the strength of Jesus's conviction.

When we allow pain and desolation and sufferings to drive us

to our knees with our face to the Father, we can experience trans-
formative periods of intense spiritual growth. When you're in the
desert, head toward Jesus and the abundant life he offers.

The dryness I refer to here comes about when we allow laziness or indifference to prevent our actively seeking to know, live,
and share our faith. This could be considered a willful dryness,
in which we don't feel the presence of God because we are not
actively seeking him. God is always waiting, but he expects us to
take steps toward him.

"Ask, and it will be given you; seek, and you will find; knock,
and it will be opened to you" (Matthew 7:7).

New Evangelizers in Action: Sarah Reinhard—Evangelizing at Home and Online

"I sin. All. The. Time," says Sarah Reinhard when asked to identify her biggest challenges in living her faith. "And I would rather be napping."

As a convert to Catholicism, Sarah also feels the pressure of having much to learn. "There isn't enough time to cram all that information into my brain," she says. "Except it isn't just information."

That doesn't stop Sarah from immersing herself in ways of knowing, living, and sharing her faith that mesh with her God-given personality. In addition to serving as her parish's webmaster, she is also the editor and designer of the parish bulletin. She writes for multiple blogs, such as CatholicMom.com and NewEvangelizers.com, and has authored several popular books about living the faith in today's world. She is delighted to see "an excitement among the laity, a ripening and maturity in my own faith walk, new resources, and especially more technologically savvy resources."

Sarah says that modern social media "make it easier for us to reach each other on a personal level in light of how very isolated so much of our lives are becoming." Her participation in the New Evangelization through blogs "has kept me in touch with people who inspire me, encourage me, and challenge me. It has planted the seeds in me to listen to God and trust that he can qualify even an imperfect instrument such as me."

You can follow Sarah online at www.SnoringScholar.com.

Mortal Combat

I'd be doing you a complete disservice if I failed to differentiate between intentional or willful dryness and the spiritual dryness that God sometimes allows in our lives. The goal of this dryness is to help us grow in faith and virtue.

It is important to recognize that many great saints experienced intense spiritual dryness in their lives. These men and women of heroic virtue made the decision to push on and push forward, despite whatever pain and obstacles (physical or spiritual) they encountered. For example, after the death of Blessed Mother Theresa of Calcutta, it was learned from her writings that she had spent a considerable amount of her life in "loneliness," "dryness," and "darkness."[4] In working through these periods of desolation, she grew in holiness.

The same holds true for us. As St. Paul wrote in Romans 5:3–5:

> We rejoice in our sufferings, knowing that suffering produces endurance, and endurance produces character, and character produces hope, and hope does not

disappoint us, because God's love has been poured into our hearts through the Holy Spirit who has been given to us.

The early disciples often experienced pain and difficulties in their efforts to evangelize the world. Acts 15:22 shows Paul and Barnabas exhorting the disciples to persevere in faith: "It is necessary for us to undergo many hardships to enter the kingdom of God."

In one of my favorite spiritual books of all time, *Dark Night of the Soul* by St. John of the Cross, the Spanish mystic explains that periods of desolation can move us to rely more deeply on God and so grow in union with him. "God leads into the dark night those whom He desires to purify from all these imperfections so that He may bring them farther onward."[5] God allows us to experience dryness so that we might develop greater virtue. Sometimes simply knowing this lessens the severity of the dryness and our difficulty in overcoming it.

In life we experience deserts of our own doing as well as dryness that God allows in order to purify and perfect us. Neither is insurmountable.

We should keep this truth at the forefront in our efforts to know our faith, live our faith, and share our faith. For if there is anything that can be certain, it is that the devil has no desire to see the Church succeed in these endeavors to re-evangelize the world for Jesus Christ. The evil one will try with all his might to discourage us from our efforts and to convince us that no consolation awaits us on the other side of the desert. "Resist him, firm in your faith, knowing that the same experience of suffering is required of your brotherhood throughout the world" (1 Peter 5:9).

Questions

1. What are some obstacles that discourage you from being a New Evangelizer?

2. When God feels distant, or when you find yourself in a desert, how does that affect the energy you put into your prayer life and living out your faith?

3. Knowing that there will be periods of dryness in your life, how can you prepare now for those moments so as to continue living in the light and joy of Christ even then?

Prayer for Help in Times of Spiritual Dryness

Lord,

in moments when my faith feels dry,

please send your Holy Spirit to inspire me.

Inspire me to repent.

Inspire me to give thanks.

Inspire me to trust.

Inspire me to hope.

In those times, Lord, when I feel you've abandoned me,

give me the certitude that you'll never abandon me

and the wisdom to see you,

especially when my faith is weak.

Amen.

chapter five
Why Sheep Get Lost

> In order to be a perfect member of a flock of sheep,
> one has to be, foremost, a sheep.
> —Albert Einstein[1]

The Billy Graham Crusade was coming to town.

Billy Graham wouldn't actually be there, but all over town, and even at our own Catholic church, everyone was buzzing about this supposedly enormous gathering being billed as a "Billy Graham Evangelistic Association" outreach, with Christian preachers and singers and comedians. Posters and flyers seemed to paper every grocery store and coffee shop I visited. Billboards along the highway advertised the event. The expectation was that thousands of souls would be saved for Jesus.

At first this meant very little to me. The only thing I knew about Billy Graham was that he was the guy who used to take over the television with his "crusades," usually on a Friday night when *The Dukes of Hazzard* was supposed to be on. I didn't have a problem with Billy Graham personally, but when I was a kid, church stuff was supposed to be reserved for Sundays, not Friday nights when I just wanted to watch car chases.

It was 2001 when the crusade came to town, before I'd made my first rosary or even considered serving God in some capacity.

For the previous few years, though, my faith life had been under-going a dramatic transformation. I was on fire for Jesus Christ like never before, but in a way that was more Protestant than Catholic.

As a cradle Catholic I had gone to Mass every Sunday, cele-brated Advent and the other seasons as they presented themselves, and said grace before each dinner. From my family and schooling I had received a foundation for my belief in God and even a fervor for the salvation offered by Jesus Christ. But the weak and theo-retical way in which I lived my own brand of Catholicism soft-ened that foundation. Really, it was wobbly and weak. The idea that the Catholic Church contained the fullness of truth simply eluded me.

For example, the Catholic Church teaches that the Eucharist is the source and summit of our faith (*CCC*, 1324, quoting Vatican II's *Lumen Gentium*, 11). In the bread and wine Jesus Christ becomes physically present to us. But despite my receiving the Eucharist nearly every Sunday of my life from second grade on, I had no clue what that meant. I would absentmindedly say, "Amen," when offered a Host, with no idea what that *Amen* was supposed to confirm. From the books and teachings I was ingesting, I had become one of the nearly 70 percent of Catholics who do not believe the Church's teaching on the real presence of Jesus Christ in the Eucharist.[2]

Now I was listening to Protestant ministers more than the priest at my local parish. The attractiveness of picking and choosing what teachings I wanted to adhere to was undeniable.

New Evangelizers in Action: Jennifer Fitz—Taking Small Steps

"I tend to be shy," says Jennifer Fitz in regard to sharing her faith. "I feel weird acting all Catholic around my less-practicing family members, like they'd feel as if I were putting on, being holier-than-thou, and so on."

So how does she work to overcome those hesitancies?

Jennifer returned to the Church in 1999. She now teaches religious education, writes for various Catholic blogs, and does her best to witness to her non-Catholic friends about the beauty of Catholicism. Continuing to find ways to know and live out her faith is a constant work in progress.

"My family was nominally Catholic, and we barely practiced the faith," she says. "I missed all that Catholic-y stuff, and even as a catechist, I feel a little awkward moving around the parish church, never quite sure if I'm reverent in the right way at the right times, things like that. I'm finally at a point where I can go to Mass every day."

When asked about the New Evangelization on the local level, Jennifer says, "I'm hoping that we can continue to make slow and steady improvements in our parish religious education program. I'm just a catechist, not Queen of Everything, but I try to do my part and help others do their part as well as they can.

"I'm thrilled with the work of so many other faithful Catholics in the New Evangelization and all the people I've met who are putting so much into sharing the faith with others and trying to grow in holiness themselves. To be trying to do my part and to have so many others also making the effort makes me want to pray, 'Lord let me be lost amid ten thousand other evangelists,' you know?"

You can read Jennifer's blog at jenniferfitz.wordpress.com.

Questioning My Catholicism

In the years when I was living well inside the Bible Belt, I was surrounded by Christian bookstores of all flavors, most with a distinctly non-Catholic array of offerings. Back in my twenties I was a regular customer of one of the bigger Protestant book chains, and one day I asked if they had any books about Catholicism.

"For or against it?" was the response I received.

"Um…for?" I stammered.

"Sorry," the clerk told me. "You'll have to go somewhere else for that."

The only publication that dealt with Catholicism in that huge store—packed from floor to ceiling with books, Bibles, and book-marks—was one written from the perspective of how to convert your Catholic friends. "Convert them to what?" I wondered. "What is wrong with being Catholic?"

It was the first time in my life that I started to wonder if maybe I belonged to the wrong faith. Had I just been blindly following my parents because of some made-up human traditions?

Despite my lack of knowledge and understanding, my desire for a greater understanding and relationship with Jesus Christ was more fervent than ever before in my life. And this was a good thing. I'd pick up just about any book with his name on the cover, no matter the source. But it seemed as if every one of them had something negative to say about the Catholic Church.

The Virgin Mary? According to some of the books I read, apparently I'd been worshipping her my whole life without even knowing it.

The *Catechism*? That was just some book of rules that a bunch of old men in Rome put together to keep me in line.

Catholics not using contraception? Again, that was how the Catholic Church kept itself rolling in the dough. If Catholics couldn't use contraception, then more Catholics would be born, and thus there would be more Catholics putting money in the collection basket. (That one makes me laugh!)

Who Needs Religion?

And now the Billy Graham Crusade was coming to town. According to local news sources, just under two hundred churches from many different denominations and ethnic backgrounds were working together to make this happen. Even our local Catholic parish got involved. Thus I decided to accept the invitation of our pastor to attend a volunteer training workshop for the upcoming event. One evening I sat in this workshop, right in our Catholic sanctuary, and watched the Protestant facilitator draw stick figures on a whiteboard.

"On this one side we have us" he said, drawing a man. "On the other side we have God." He drew a much larger stick figure.

"In between us and God, we have a deep chasm," he went on, drawing a deep canyon between the figures. "This chasm, this rift between us and God, is caused by our sinfulness."

My fellow Catholic parishioners nodded in affirmation, and I nodded along with them.

"How do we bridge this rift between us and God?" he asked. "How do we get from here," he circled the human stick figure, "over to here?" He then circled the God stick figure.

"One answer," he said, and he drew a cross in the chasm. The horizontal arms of the cross reached from the stick-figure man to the stick-figure God. "Only Jesus Christ, who gave his life on the cross, can bridge the gap between us and God."

Again we all nodded in full agreement. But then the facilitator said something that to this day shakes me to my core.

"No religion can help you get to God," he said. "Only Jesus Christ can do that, and Jesus Christ requires no religion. Only faith."

If I'd been driving a car at that moment, my feet would have slammed on the brakes. No religion? What did he mean by that?

Keep in mind, I was sitting right in the church I'd gone to for years. My wife and I had been married in this Catholic church. And right in front of us next to the altar was the tabernacle with the real presence of Jesus Christ inside, a fact that admittedly eluded me at the time. Because of my own lack of understanding of my lifelong faith, at that very moment I took the largest step away from Catholicism that I would ever take in my life. I wanted to serve God in whatever way he wanted, but here this man was standing in our Catholic sanctuary telling me that my religion would not get me to God. The only way to do it would be through Jesus.

But wasn't Jesus present in the Catholic Church? Then what was the problem? What did all of this mean? And again, all of the questions that had been coming to the surface through books and tapes offered testimony to the fact that I was apparently wasting my time with Catholicism when there was a seemingly much easier path to God.

Undeniably, the people behind this event were on fire for Jesus.

I was on fire for Jesus. My fellow Catholics were on fire for Jesus. My pastor was on fire for Jesus. And maybe the gentleman leading our training class had simply strayed from the script provided by the Billy Graham Association. But the question still had to be asked: How was it possible for all of us to be focused on the same goal but disagree on so many critical items directly related to reaching the goal?

Interestingly enough, I have the Billy Graham Evangelistic Association to thank for bringing me closer to Jesus Christ through the Church he established. But this man had just said that no religion would help me get to God, and at that moment I was prepared to leave my faith.

Hindsight, fortunately, offers greater levels of clarity. Now, years later, I can see multiple problems that were at work at that point. My lack of knowledge of my faith, my not actually living out my Catholic faith in a sacramental way, my desire to share Jesus with others but sharing the wrong truth—not the fullness—all of these came to a head.

I wanted to be a part of a massive evangelization effort for Jesus Christ and the good of the whole world. I have no doubt that that was the goal of the good people from the Billy Graham Evangelistic Association as well. But I had no rebuttal that night for the facilitator's proposal that religion was unnecessary. I had no answer to that claim.

I was totally unfit to be reaching out and attempting to share my faith with others. I didn't have a firm foundation and comprehension of my own faith. How could I attempt to evangelize others?

Evangelization was needed, for sure. *I* needed to be more fully evangelized before venturing into the world to evangelize others.

Mass Exodus

I suspect that the confusion I was experiencing is what leads most so-called "former Catholics" to walk away from their faith. They leave before they have a chance to really understand the whats and whys of Catholic Church teachings at a meaningful level.

Let's start with the basics.

Do you go to Mass on Sundays? Excellent.

What about *every* Sunday?

If yes, then congratulations. You are a part of the very elite 23 percent of U.S. Catholics who actually attend Mass each and every week. That's the percentage that the Center for Applied Research in the Apostolate (CARA) came to in a 2008 survey.[3]

I can understand the difficulty of juggling priorities in life. In between a whole gaggle of kids, various apostolates, radio and podcast and video programs to produce, and trying to pick up extra work here and there to keep the children fed, it's hard to accomplish everything I'd like to in life. Again, there are excuses aplenty. But some areas of our faith lives are simply mandatory, and Mass is one of them.

Now, one might offer the explanation "Well, those people who don't come are just cafeteria Catholics," or, "The source of that study has an agenda against the Church, so the numbers are probably skewed." I've heard both of these responses and many like them. And I stop myself and others from using them, for they don't get to the heart of the problem.

There's something to be learned from such studies, no matter how much or how little credence you give the source. Even if the study is inaccurate, even if Church attendance is actually 80 percent, it still leaves the question, "Why don't we see 100 percent participation at Mass each and every Sunday?" After all, the third commandment says, "Remember to keep holy the Sabbath day." That means, unless you've got a seriously grave reason, it's a seriously grave sin to miss Mass.

The fact that people are missing Mass at all should make us realize that there's a very good chance that they don't fully understand what it means to participate in the worship of God in the Catholic Church. Something is missing here.

In another study from CARA, the six main reasons why Catholics stop attending Mass include:

1. busy schedules or lack of time
2. family responsibilities
3. health problems or disabilities
4. conflicts with work
5. not believing that missing Mass is a sin
6. not seeing themselves as religious people.[4]

No matter what reason people give, they need to be asked a more basic question: "Do you have a personal relationship with Jesus Christ?"

Some people may avoid responding to that question, especially if someone bent on trashing the Catholic Church has directed it at them. They may anticipate a barrage of other questions that can intimidate the ill-prepared Catholic: "Why do you worship saints and statues?" "Why can't you pray to Jesus instead of Mary?" "Why do you worship a cracker?" "Why do you keep sacrificing Jesus every Sunday?" These questions illustrate the myriad misunderstandings people have about Catholicism.

Nevertheless, if people don't go to Mass because they're too busy, they don't think missing Mass is a sin, or they're "just not very religious," there's a big red flag waving in the wind that probably indicates that Jesus is not a part—or at least not the center—of their daily existence. If people do not understand the importance of Jesus Christ in their lives, they most likely will not understand the critical and life-changing essence of Jesus Christ physically present in the sacrament of the Eucharist.

I believe wholeheartedly that if people truly understood the Catholic Church's teachings on the Eucharist—that Communion is not just a symbol but is Jesus Christ physically present, Body, Blood, soul, and divinity—then it would be *impossible* to walk away from the Catholic faith. Because if people understood that in the Eucharist we have the source and summit of our faith— meaning, everything we come from (the source) and everything we're journeying toward (the summit)—there is no way someone could abandon that. Catholics who make the Eucharist the center of their lives make Jesus the center of their lives.

How many former Catholics do you know who genuinely understand and believe that? I'd guess zero.

There may be legitimate circumstances that keep people from regularly attending Mass, especially health problems and disabilities. Someone in financial difficulties might only find employment that requires work on Sundays. Still, in that 23 percent of Catholics who never miss Mass, I'm certain you'll find Catholics in ill health and Catholics who must work on Sundays. They find a way to attend Mass because they've made the Eucharist the center of their lives. And without the center, they know that their lives will be off balance.

When people stop attending Mass regularly, there's a good chance they may just walk away from the Church all together. What are some of the common reasons people give for leaving the Catholic Church or even abandoning the Christian faith?

The Litany of Excuses

From my time on radio, as well as through social networking sites like Facebook, I've compiled a fairly comprehensive list of reasons why people leave the Catholic Church. Keep in mind that these are excuses given, and they may or may not be correct or justified. As you read them, ask yourself if you know people who have given these responses. Perhaps write their names next to the reason and keep them in prayer. Ask the Holy Spirit to strengthen you and to give you courage and the wisdom to counter whatever excuse someone has to the faith.

In the off chance that one of these excuses is the same as a thought you're currently entertaining, please know that the Church has provided beautiful, thought-provoking, and life-changing answers to each and every one of these oppositions. Are you willing to go looking for the answers?

So here's my list:

- poor catechesis (religious education)
- not enough Catholics taking ownership of their faith
- misunderstanding of Catholic practices and teachings (for example, "too much emphasis on worshipping saints and statues")
- not wanting to be accountable
- no role models in the Church
- non-Catholic spouse

THE NEW EVANGELIZATION AND YOU

- kids want to go to the "fun" church down the street
- too much anti-Catholic information distributed online and in the world
- disagreement with Church teachings (usually in regard to premarital sex, divorce, homosexuality, contraception, and other "pelvic issues," as some former Catholics like to call them)
- traumatic or bad experience with a Church leader
- inability to forgive wrongdoings of some Church leaders or members
- things changing (for example, implementation of Vatican II documents and the *Third Roman Missal*)
- Mass is old-fashioned and doesn't speak to today's issues
- parents drop off kids at religious education but don't actually take part in Church
- Church is too structured
- Church is too conservative
- Church is too liberal
- Church is too involved in politics
- Church isn't involved enough in politics
- got divorced and remarried and no longer feel welcome
- all the Church wants is money
- the priest sex scandal and pedophilia
- the Church refuses to change with the times
- the Catholic Church is becoming more Protestant
- prefer belief in *sola fide* (faith alone) and *sola scriptura* (Scripture alone)
- priest is _____ (a jerk, too fluffy, too loud, too quiet, boring, wrong, uninspiring, and so on)

- don't get anything out of Mass
- no fellowship at the parish
- the music is horrible
- not enough Bible study
- not enough ministries
- not enough childcare
- not enough doughnuts
- the religious education teachers are terrible
- I don't want to have more babies, but the Catholic Church says I have to
- I don't like the way the Church looks
- too many statues
- not enough statues
- other churches have more social opportunities
- it's too hard to take my kids to Mass
- Catholics say they're open to life, but they scowl at my kids if they make a peep
- it's easier to be Protestant
- don't know the history of the Catholic Church and the early Church fathers
- the Bible doesn't support Catholicism
- we weren't allowed to read the Bible
- indifference
- any Church is fine as long as it is Christian
- I believe priests should be allowed to marry
- I believe women should be allowed to be priests
- priests aren't approachable
- the local Catholic church is too far away
- people are too self-centered and not interested in Jesus

- behavior of clergy—not the sex scandals but the "I am the priest/bishop" attitude
- people won't miss me if I leave anyway
- my wants got in the way of my needs
- lack of warmth from the parish
- homilies are out of touch with the real world
- lack of emphasis on a relationship with Jesus Christ
- I don't want to be part of organized religion
- no offerings for young adults
- I keep getting asked for money and to volunteer
- I don't believe in confession
- too many rules to follow
- mishandling of funds by the Church (parish, diocese, and so on), including donations made toward seemingly political or other questionable causes
- the Church is full of hypocrites
- the extraordinary ministers aren't worthy to be distributing Communion
- I went to college and just drifted away
- I went to college and there wasn't a good Catholic ministry
- lack of understanding of what the Church believes and teaches and why.

I never received the response "I don't believe Jesus is in the Eucharist." Again, if we keep our eyes on Jesus Christ, leaving is never an option.

Questions

1. How well do you know your Catholic faith?
2. Have you ever thought about leaving the Catholic Church, or did you leave the Church? If so, what made you stay or come back?
3. What area of Catholicism would you be the most nervous about trying to explain to a non-Catholic or fallen-away Catholic?
4. What are some action steps you can take to better understand that area?

Prayer to Know God Better

Lord,

I don't know you as well as I ought,

nor do I love you as much as I could.

But I offer myself to you once again, Lord—

that you would take my strengths along with my weaknesses,

my confidence as well as my doubts,

my eagerness as well as my laziness,

and in all things redirect me to you.

I long to know you, live for you, and serve you,

but I need your help to do it right.

Amen.

chapter six

A Basic Definition of Catholicism

> Don't take life too seriously. You'll never get out of it
> alive.
> —BUGS BUNNY, *Rabbits Feat*

I've spent several years in media ministry—producing video series, writing books and articles, creating podcasts, and even spending three hours a day on live talk radio discussing our Catholic faith. But if someone asked, "Hey, what is Catholicism?" I'd probably stammer and stumble like the next guy as I tried to fit two thousand years of teaching, history, theology, and witness into a 140-character tweetable answer.

It may seem like a silly question, akin to asking a chef, "What is cooking?" But if someone were to ask you what Catholicism is, would you be able to answer somewhat succinctly? Again, in today's Twitter-influenced world, the reality is that many people have little patience for long answers. So how would you quickly explain Catholicism—before your listener tunes out?

There's the technical definition of Catholicism, which covers the faith, practice, and hierarchy of the Roman Catholic Church. This includes Christian doctrine that is specifically Catholic in nature, as opposed to common beliefs that are also held by

Protestants and the Eastern Orthodox. But that doesn't explain what Catholicism *is*.

The *Catechism* says that the Catholic Church is "the Church established by Christ on the foundation of the Apostles, possessing the fullness of the means of salvation which he has willed: correct and complete confession of faith, full sacramental life, and ordained ministry in apostolic succession" (CCC, glossary). A further explanation is that the Catholic Church possesses the four characteristics that we proclaim each time we recite the Nicene Creed. That is, the Catholic Church is one, holy, catholic (meaning "universal"), and apostolic (see CCC, 811, citing *Lumen Gentium*, 8).

Given that one of the primary aspects of the New Evangelization is taking the opportunity to be re-evangelized ourselves, to take advantage of learning about our faith throughout our whole lives, this is a great place to start. Though we've most likely professed these four marks of the Church hundreds if not thousands of times throughout our lives, do we really know the meaning of the words we're saying? What do these four marks mean, and why are they so vitally important?

Knowing and understanding these four marks made all the difference to me in my late twenties, when I started asking, "Why am I Catholic?" and, "Why does the Catholic Church teach what it teaches?" I ended up falling in love with my faith more deeply than I could have ever imagined.

One Is Not the Loneliest Number
Having lived in the Bible Belt for most of my life, I've heard countless people referring to "the Church" without even taking Catholicism into consideration. The understanding is that "the

Church" or "the body of Christ" is simply anyone who is a Christian.

But Scripture tells a different story. In Ephesians 4:4–6, St. Paul writes, "There is *one* body and *one* Spirit, just as you were called to the *one* hope that belongs to your call, *one* Lord, *one* faith, *one* baptism, *one* God and Father of us all" (emphasis mine).

Doesn't it strike you as odd that there are so many references to oneness and yet we live in a world where the Reformation splintered Christianity into anywhere between five thousand and forty thousand different denominations, depending on how they're counted?[1] After fifteen hundred years of oneness (save exceptions like the separation of our Orthodox brethren in 1054), now there are so many different branches and offshoots that many people give very little consideration to Catholicism as the original Church founded by Jesus Christ. And yet it is. That Church, for fifteen hundred years, was *one*, just as Christ wished it to be.

"And I have other sheep, that are not of this fold; I must bring them also, and they will heed my voice. So there shall be one flock, one shepherd" (John 10:16).

The Church Jesus Christ established was not supposed to contain thousands or tens of thousands of fractured offshoots. The original Church established by Jesus Christ is the Catholic Church. It is the one Church that contains the fullness of faith, Scripture and Tradition, the rich history of teachings and the saints, and so much more.

It's easy to wonder what God must think about the extreme divisions that exist among believers today. At some point some person thought that he knew better than the Catholic Church and went off and started his own thing. That is, in fact, what Martin

Luther did at the outset of the Protestant Reformation. But then what happened? Well, obviously, someone at some point came up with ideas about Scripture and theology that conflicted with Luther's, and then yet another split occurred. This phenomenon of Christians acting as their own self-appointed popes and magisteriums led to one fracture after another.

How does that possibly match the Nicene Creed and Jesus's own prayer "that they may all be one; even as you, Father, are in me, and I in you, that they also may be in us, so that the world may believe that you have sent me" (John 17:21)?

For two thousand years there has been *one* Catholic Church that Jesus Christ himself proclaimed the gates of hell would not overcome (see Matthew 16:18). It is imperative to understand that it was always his intention that we all be one in the Church, to which he entrusted the world.

New Evangelizers in Action: Ryan Eggenberger—Working Within the Parish

"I think I have the tools I need and the courage I need, but I am continually thrown off by the assumptions and misinformation that people begin with," says Ryan Eggenberger, a convert in his mid-twenties, when talking about sharing his faith. "Like never once questioning contraception; where do you even start when trying to evangelize about that?"

It can be frustrating to share your faith with a misinformed world, but Ryan, on fire for his faith, doesn't let that stop him. He has found like-minded persons at his parish in the archdiocese of Detroit.

"Our Lady of Good Counsel in Plymouth, Michigan, is active," Ryan says. "We are big in social media and getting free resources out to every parish member. This weekend we handed out free copies of Dr. Janet Smith's *Contraception: Why Not?* talk, which she gave at our parish last year.⁴ We have one handout like that a month, it seems."

When asked about roadblocks to the New Evangelization, Ryan mentions parishes he's visited where "the priests [are] not…willing to try anything new or not understanding the vitality of new media and its effect on virtually every generation. Most priests are not on social media, so they don't understand."

For the New Evangelization, though, Ryan is hopeful.

"We need to take it to the next level," he says. "Give people tangible ways to start those conversations with others about the gospel. Let's get Bibles and rosaries out to folks. We do a lot of talking about the 'new springtime,' but it's not going to happen just by listening to podcasts, unless we can take that information and share it with others. There are many of us who are ready to spread the gospel like wildfire but need more resources to make that happen."

You can visit Ryan's personal website at www.RyanEggenberger.com.

Holy in Our Head

I've got good news and bad news when it comes to the second mark of the Church.

The bad news is that we mere humans are full of sin and totally unworthy of salvation, and on our own we completely mess up. I'm a sinner, you're a sinner, your priest is a sinner, that nun in the convent is a sinner, and even the pope is a sinner. At times in our lives we absolutely reek of sin.

The good news is that Jesus Christ is the head of the Church and we are *one* body of Christ. Given the fact that Christ is sinless and blameless and therefore *holy*, then by that very definition the Church is holy.

But how is that possible, given that the Church is full of stinky sinners? The *Catechism* tells us:

> This is because Christ, the Son of God, who with the Father and the Spirit is hailed as "alone holy," loved the Church as his Bride, giving himself up for her so as to sanctify her; he joined her to himself as his body and endowed her with the gift of the Holy Spirit for the glory of God. (CCC, 823, quoting *Lumen Gentium*, 39)

Christ died on the cross for the forgiveness of our sins. By his death and resurrection, we are redeemed. Moreover, he joins us to himself, letting us share his holiness.

The early Church, the Church of the apostles, was also holy despite its being full of sinners. That should give you some comfort, especially if you sometimes feel as if you're a no-good louse who could never help anyone else grow closer to God because you're not even capable of getting it right yourself! If you ever feel that way, keep in mind that that pretty much defines every Christian who has ever lived. Yet the Church remains holy because Christ is her head.

> All members of the Church, including her ministers, must acknowledge that they are sinners. In everyone, the weeds of sin will still be mixed with the good wheat of the Gospel until the end of time. Hence the Church gathers sinners already caught up in Christ's salvation but still

THE NEW EVANGELIZATION AND YOU

on the way to holiness (CCC, 827; see 1 John 1:8–10; Matthew 13:24–30).

The Church, led by Jesus Christ and guided by his Holy Spirit, provides each of us the means to achieve holiness. The sacraments give the graces necessary to strengthen us in our spiritual journey to sainthood. Jesus gives them to us, through the Church, for the sole purpose of making us holy. Nowhere else are they offered in their fullness.

The sacraments are interdependent, as established by Jesus. For example, we cannot have the sacrament of the Eucharist, which brings us healing and strength, if not for the sacrament of holy orders. The ordained priests act *in persona Christi* (in the person of Christ) to provide that nourishing feast. The sacrament of holy orders also allows for the sacrament of reconciliation, which reunites us with God after our sins separate us from his embrace.

Universal Soldiers

My favorite of the four marks of the Church established by Jesus Christ is that it's universal. The reason it's my favorite is because it's the easiest one to explain.

The word *Catholic* means, in Greek, "universal." When you think "universal," perhaps your first thought is that it pertains to the whole universe. Or maybe it's something that applies to the whole world. Sticking with this definition alone, you'll do just fine. In fact, for many years I explained this mark of universality by saying (somewhat simplistically though not erroneously) that if you were to go to Mass on any Sunday anywhere in the world, you'd hear the same Scripture readings.

But the word *universal*, when applied to Catholicism, has a deeper meaning. *Universal* in terms of Catholicism means "according to the totality" or "in keeping with the whole" (*CCC*, 830). In other words, the Church affects everything totally and completely.

Imagine an area of our world, of your very existence, that isn't somehow affected by the Catholic Church. Governments, educational institutions, businesses, families, social programs—all are rooted in various teachings of the Catholic Church and are orchestrated by members of the body of Christ.

There's a popular game, with origins on the Internet, called "Six Degrees of Kevin Bacon." The object is to name a motion picture celebrity and then figure out how many "degrees" away from Kevin Bacon that actor is, based on the movies the actor has appeared in. For example, Jack Nicholson is one degree from Kevin Bacon because he starred in *A Few Good Men* (1992) with Kevin Bacon. Elvis Presley has a Bacon Number of two because he was in the movie *Change of Habit* (1969) with Edward Asner, and Edward Asner was in *JFK* (1991) with Kevin Bacon. The premise is that any celebrity can be tied to a Kevin Bacon film within six "degrees" or films.

Now, just about everything and everyone is within one degree of the Catholic Church because of the distinct effects that the Church has had on the world. Whether you know a Catholic, are a Catholic, went to a Catholic school, or lived near a Catholic church, it's borderline impossible not to be affected in some way by the Catholic Church. That's universality.

What's even more pertinent to the mark of universality is the challenge that is attached to it for each of us. *Lumen Gentium* states, "The character of universality which adorns the People of God is a gift from the Lord himself whereby the Catholic Church ceaselessly and efficaciously seeks for the return of all humanity and all its goods under Christ the Head in the unity of his Spirit."[2]

Again, as far back as the Council of Nicea in AD 325, when the Creed was being agreed upon, there was the idea of universality. The Church is calling all to a greater and deeper unity with God. That is a call for ongoing re-evangelization.

As a side note, Kevin Bacon and his brother were once guests on the talk show my wife and I hosted on satellite radio. So that means I'm one degree from Kevin Bacon. And since you're reading this book, that gives you a Bacon number of two.

Apostolic
While the universal mark of the Church established by Jesus Christ is the one with which I can most relate, the final mark is the one that had the greatest impact upon me in terms of accepting my faith. I take great stock in history. I wouldn't consider myself a historian or history buff by any stretch of the imagination, but I do enjoy the logic of evaluating lessons past generations have learned and applying them to the present. As the oft-repeated adage from the poet George Santayana's *Reason in Common Sense* says, "Those who cannot remember the past are condemned to repeat it."[3]

From a Catholic perspective, "Those who do not fully understand the early Church are at risk of losing the fullness of the faith."

Going back to my early thirties, shortly after my wife actually converted to Catholicism and I was still wondering whether it was necessary to adhere to its tenets, I was running errands one fall evening, and I prayed out loud as I drove. "Why should I believe any of this stuff, God? It's so much easier to just love you and do my own thing rather than to try to follow all of these ridiculous rules."

I got so frustrated; I actually pulled into a grocery store parking lot and called my parents. It was my mom and dad, after all, who brought me up Catholic. Surely they'd be able to answer my questions.

When my mother answered the phone, I suspect she quickly wished she hadn't.

"Why should I pay attention to all these old guys in Rome, Mom? What do they know about being married, or having a regular job, or dealing with all the garbage I have to deal with every day? Why should I pay attention to Jesus's mom? Why can't I just focus on Jesus?"

My poor mother, also a cradle Catholic, stammered on the other end of the line, "I'm not sure."

I hung up the phone disillusioned but not ready to stop asking the hard-hitting questions I'd neglected to ask throughout my life.

In the weeks that followed, I started doing something I'd never done before: I sought out answers to the question "Why am I Catholic?" My search led me for the first time to the early fathers and mothers of the Church, the great men and women who either knew Jesus Christ personally or were Christians in the first four centuries after his death and resurrection. How did those Christians live out their faith? Did they go to confession? Did they celebrate Mass? What did they believe back then, and how did it compare with the Catholic Church of today? If those early Christians followed the apostles, the original disciples of Jesus Christ, and adhered to their teachings, wouldn't logic predicate that today's Church should adhere to those same teachings?

In looking at these early Christians, I found myself absolutely awestruck at discovering for the first time that "those old guys in Rome" can actually be traced back, as if on a family tree, to the apostles. Our current pope can trace his position back to St. Peter, our very first pope, to whom Jesus Christ said,

> You are Peter, and on this rock I will build my Church, and the gates of Hades shall not prevail against it. I will give you the keys of the kingdom of heaven, and whatever you bind on earth shall be bound in heaven, and whatever you loose on earth shall be loosed in heaven. (Matthew 16:18–19)

After years of being Catholic without actually understanding my faith, I could see in a concrete way that this was the faith of the apostles. And if it was the faith of the apostles, right down to the celebration of the Mass and the lineage of the popes, then I could have absolute confidence in its teaching authority as it stands today. I have absolute confidence that adhering to the authority given to Christ's apostles and handed down through the generations will bring me closer to Jesus Christ.

Simple Questions, Simple Answers

In my online and media ministry, the most common tale I hear from fallen-away Catholics starts with, "I went to Catholic school from kindergarten through twelfth grade." It's gotten to the point that when someone tells me that, I automatically assume the person is no longer Catholic!

Occasionally people will add additional comments to validate their Catholic experience:

"I was an altar boy."

"I went to Catholic college too."

"I memorized Latin."

"The priest was a mean old man."

"No one ever talked about having a personal relationship with Jesus."

"I never once heard a Catholic read from the Bible."

Those last two comments always make me shake my head in sadness and frustration. How can you say Catholics don't have a relationship with Jesus when every Sunday Mass revolves around the celebration of the sacrifice Jesus made for us and presents to us in the Eucharist? And how can you say that Catholics don't read the Bible, when every Sunday Mass includes a reading from the Old Testament, a responsorial Psalm, a reading from the New Testament, a Gospel reading, and multiple uses of Scripture in the prayers and responses said by the priest and the congregation?

Alas, the overall view of the Catholic Church for many fallen-away Catholics is based upon the personal experiences they may have had at a perhaps lackluster parish or with a particular priest who had the unapproachable personality of an angry mobster or the milquetoast delivery of Ben Stein (the guy from *Ferris Bueller's Day Off* who drones on and on in a dreary, monotonous voice). Some seem to hate the Church. But Archbishop Fulton Sheen was well known for saying, "There are not one hundred people in the United States who hate the Catholic Church, but there are millions who hate what they wrongly perceive the Catholic Church to be."

I hope this chapter has helped you understand Catholicism. If someone asks you to explain the faith, try saying,

> Catholicism is belonging to the Church established by
> Jesus Christ, which is one body and one Spirit (Ephesians

4:4) and one flock guided by one shepherd (John 10:16). Catholicism is universal in that it is the only Christian church that affects the entire world in every way. It is holy by the mere fact that Christ, who is all-holy, is the head and founder of our Church. And the Catholic Church is apostolic in that it is the only Church that can trace itself back to St. Peter, whose authority was given by Jesus Christ.

Understand the four marks of the Church—one, holy, catholic, and apostolic—for they form the framework for deeper understanding of the authority of the Church, the Eucharist, confession, the priesthood, marriage, family, and more.

If the above definition is too long to commit to memory, then perhaps you can ask and answer the following for your questioner:

• Did Jesus establish the Church and give authority to his apostles to act in his name and in his place? Yes.

• Did he promise to send the Holy Spirit to guide the Church after his ascension into heaven? Yes.

• If you believe these things and yet do not acknowledge Catholicism as the Church to which Jesus called us all to belong, then at what point did the Holy Spirit abandon the Church? The answer is that he never did. And he never will.

Questions

1. How do you describe Catholicism to someone who is unfamiliar with it?
2. When you define Catholicism, do you think of areas where you could improve your understanding of the faith, improve

the way you live the faith, and improve the way you share the faith?

3. Of the four marks of the Church (one, holy, catholic, and apostolic), which speaks to you the most personally, and why?

Prayer for Understanding of the Faith

Lord,

I thank you for my faith,

and I thank you for the Catholic Church.

Please help me to have a better understanding of the four marks of the Church.

Help me understand what it means to be one.

Help me understand what it means to be holy.

Help me understand what it means to be catholic.

And help me understand what it means to be apostolic.

And through this better understanding,

please help me live the faith each day,

so that others may be drawn to you

through the light they see shining from me.

Amen.

chapter seven
Accepting the Mission

> You keep using that word. I do not think it means
> what you think it means.
> —MANDY PATINKIN as Inigo Montoya, *The Princess
> Bride*

I sometimes wonder if I'd be as in love with the Catholic faith as I am if not for the Internet.

My wife and I got married in 1995, right when the Internet was really taking off. America Online, Compuserve, Prodigy, and a few other subscription start-ups offered various levels of Internet access, and within a couple months of moving into our first apartment, we felt like trailblazers when we signed up with an independent Internet service provider and installed a second phone line pretty much dedicated to Internet access.

At that time I wasn't the best at practicing my faith. Not one of my web searches had anything to do with Catholicism. But I could barely imagine not being Catholic. It was practically a part of my DNA.

Jennifer, however, did not have any connection to any faith at that time. Though she was baptized Catholic, her parents withdrew from the Church just weeks prior to Jennifer's First

Communion, and for the next decade her family attended a non-denominational Christian church that didn't exactly hold Catholicism in the greatest of favor. In her late teens Jennifer's relationship with God (what little existed) further eroded to the point of nearly ceasing to exist. I came into her life a few years later. Once we decided to marry, I was the one who absolutely insisted that it be in the Church.

Though we did marry in the Catholic Church and actually went through all of the required pre-Cana sessions, we really didn't know what we were getting ourselves into. In the year or so after our wedding, I attempted to go to Mass most Sundays and felt God pulling us both closer to him. But beyond the spotty Mass attendance, I did little to cultivate that relationship. I still had no more than an eighth-grade understanding of Catholicism (which explains how I could rationalize the occasional skipping of Mass).

Yet I hoped and prayed that Jennifer would eventually feel drawn to the Catholic Church as well. She would often attend Mass with me—though, as she explained to me later, she was often put off by what she perceived as pomp and circumstance and flashiness within Catholic churches.

So Who's a Pagan Baby?

Upon discovering that our first child would be joining our family, our awareness of our need for God intensified. We engaged in countless discussions about God's place in our lives. Jennifer, having distanced herself from God for several years, doubted whether God would even welcome her back. This brought up questions about the nature of forgiveness—specifically, God's willingness to forgive even the most grievous of sins.

We also discussed baptism. I believed in infant baptism, of course, whereas Jennifer believed that baptism should be a personal decision made in adulthood.

The most interesting aspect of all these conversations was the realization not of how much Jennifer misunderstood Catholicism but of how inadequate my own knowledge was. My attempts to defend and explain it often fell flat.

One evening when Jennifer was several months pregnant, the conversation about baptism came up once again. Jennifer was visibly frustrated with my desire that our child be baptized when he or she was born.

"I don't understand why you have difficulty with this," I told her.

"It's just that I'm uncomfortable with our baby being baptized in the Catholic Church," she responded.

"But I'm Catholic! Are you bothered that I was baptized in the Catholic Church?"

She struggled to find words to clearly express what she was thinking.

"Well," she began, "aren't...well, aren't Catholics pagans?"

I'm not one to allow my jaw to drop in surprise, but I could probably have used a shovel to scoop it off the ground that evening.

"Pagans?" I repeated in disbelief. I wasn't even sure what she meant by that. "You think I'm a pagan? What does that even mean?"

"Well, that's what I remember being taught at the church I went to after my parents left the Catholic Church."

"Pagan?" I repeated. "And you still married me?"

This was one of the first moments in my life when someone called my Catholic faith into question, and my own wife was the one doing it. This was the woman I had married in the *Catholic* Church after going through *Catholic* marriage preparation. I was dumbfounded, to say the least.

I didn't own a *Catechism* at that time, and I don't think I even knew that the modern *Catechism*, promulgated and printed just a few years before, in 1992, existed. I had no idea where to look to find a rebuttal to my wife's claim that she had married a pagan. Furthermore, I actually found myself questioning my wife's character a little bit. She was willing to marry me despite her belief that I was a pagan! I tend to think now that neither of us knew what a pagan was, no more than either of us could adequately explain what Catholicism taught.

This is when the Internet became one of the greatest gifts to our marriage, as well as to our own individual relationships with Jesus Christ. That evening I sat down at my computer, dialed into the Internet, brought up a web browser, and did a search for "Are Catholics pagans?"

Amazingly, fifteen years later, when I type that same question into Google, the same page is returned as the number-one result. Asking that question online led me to a tract from Catholic Answers entitled "Is Catholicism Pagan?"[1]

I printed out the article, took it to Jennifer in the living room, and read several of the points out loud. After that I went back to that website and printed out a tract about infant baptism, then another on "What *Catholic* Means." Then one more tract after another appeared. It was as if a floodgate of information was opened for the first time in my life.

New Evangelizers in Action: Jason Elizondo and Austin Catholic New Media

In the diocese of Austin, a new breed of Catholic has been forming. In the middle of a hotbed of a growing technology industry, a group of excited young Catholics have mobilized to be of service to their local community and the world at large, using their God-given skills and resources.

Seeking a way to work with their diocese and the local radio station, Jason Elizondo and several colleagues formed Austin Catholic New Media, which is dedicated to bringing the Good News of Jesus Christ into the world through social media. The particular focus is on Catholics in the diocese, of which there are nearly 108,000 families.[5]

Oftentimes God takes small efforts into better and unexpected directions. "Austin Catholic New Media is really taking the lead for the diocese when it comes to the New Evangelization," Jason says. "Our goal is to be the home base for all Catholic new media content coming out of the diocese of Austin, as well as to give the Catholics of the diocese a voice that is lacking in our community."

Like many people his age, Jason is engaged in New Evangelization efforts in part to help others but also to bolster his own faith development.

"In the past six years I've learned more about my faith than in the prior thirty years," Jason says. "Like the servant given the talents by his Lord (Matthew 25:14–30), I feel the duty to share what I've learned. I have a responsibility to share it."

One obstacle Jason faces in living his faith is that "most of my close friends and family members are either non-practicing Catholics or nominal Catholics. So being the practicing Catholic of the group, it's sometimes difficult to be the light in the darkness, so to speak."

Despite this, his passion for sharing the faith comes in varied ways. In fact, at times he has to counter his enthusiasm for evangelizing with temperance. "The biggest challenge I face in sharing my faith is trying to evangelize without beating people over the head with it," says Jason.

You can see the good work being done by Austin Catholic New Media at their website, www.austincnm.com.

An Important Question

Why are you Catholic?

Has anyone ever asked you that question before? And if so, what emotions did you feel at that moment? Fear? Excitement? A challenge?

If you're not Catholic (yet), then why do you belong to whatever church or belief system you belong to?

Do you know the history of the Catholic Church beyond the way our modern secular society tries to portray it? By the way, in case you got your Catholic Church history from modern-day suspense novels and movies, the Church is *not* run by secret societies with albino assassin monks.

What about other aspects of Church history? Do you know when the Church was established and who established it? Do you know who gave the Catholic Church its teaching authority and how that authority operates? Do you know where to go to get a core understanding of the faith? What references are available to you?

It wasn't until I was frustrated over various issues in my life that I asked, "Why am I a part of this Church?" And along with that question, I also asked why the Church teaches so many of the things it does.

For many people, when they do have questions about their faith, finding the answers is a burdensome chore. Maybe that has been the case for you at some point in your life, or perhaps that's even the case in your life right now. But if you're asking questions, it is also necessary to ask yourself—honestly—if you're willing to really seek answers. Are you willing to invest the time and the energy? What is it you hope to discover? Why are *you* Catholic, and what do you hope to get out of your faith?

There are lots of ways to find out more about the Catholic faith. The Internet worked for me. There are also lots of good Catholic books and magazines, videos, and radio programs out there. Check out my list in chapter ten: "Fifty-two Ways to Know Your Faith." Maybe some will work for you.

Our Baptism Makes Us Evangelizers

It took getting married and becoming a father before I even started to think about my faith. My calling to be an evangelizer, a witness in this world, started long before that. And if you've been baptized, you already have a call to be an evangelizer.

Despite my wife's initial struggle with infant baptism, we did get little Sam baptized. My wife and I went on to present our four other children for baptism in their infancy. The necessity and efficacy of this sacrament of initiation eluded us for quite some time, however. Our knowledge about sacramental life was incomplete and immature.

Like many parents, we considered baptism to be more of a ritual than "the basis of the whole Christian life, the gateway to life in the Spirit…, and the door which gives access to the other sacraments" (CCC, 1213). Baptism frees us from original sin and makes us adopted children of God, members of the Church, and disciples called to witness. "As many of you as were baptized into Christ have put on Christ" (Galatians 3:27). We who are baptized are truly part of the body of Christ.

In an article entitled, "Fulfilling the Call to Evangelize," author Ann Schneible wrote, "The call to evangelize, a call received by each and every Christian at his or her baptism, is founded upon the true event of Jesus Christ's rising from the dead."[2] The waters of baptism symbolize death, specifically the death of Jesus Christ on the cross. We rise from the waters of baptism as Christ rose glorified from death.

> We were buried therefore with him by baptism into death,
> so that as Christ was raised from the dead by the glory of
> the Father, we too might live in newness of life. (Romans
> 6:4)

It is important for a New Evangelizer to understand baptism because of the two principal effects that the sacrament presents: "purification from sins and new birth in the Holy Spirit" (CCC, 1262). Jesus said, "Truly, truly, I say to you, unless one is born of water and the Spirit, he cannot enter the kingdom of God" (John 3:5). And on the day of Pentecost, St. Peter proclaimed, "Repent, and be baptized every one of you, in the name of Jesus Christ for the forgiveness of sins; and you shall receive the gift of the Holy Spirit" (Acts 2:38).

For years I focused only on the first effect of baptism. If someone asked me, "What does baptism do?" my Catholic-grade-school knowledge kicked in and I answered, "Forgives original sin."

But in the New Evangelization, and in your very life, the second promise is vitally important: If you have been baptized, *you have received the gift of the Holy Spirit.* And if you haven't been baptized, you should want to be for that reason alone.

The Holy Spirit seals the new Christian with "the indelible spiritual mark (*character*) of his belonging to Christ" (CCC, 1272), and nothing can ever remove that mark. If you were baptized as a child and went off and committed the most horrendous of sins, that mark was not erased. If you're striving to live in concert with the will of God, the Holy Spirit strengthens you to be a witness to others. The light of Christ, who has sealed you with his mark, shines through you.

What Next?

Unfortunately, many people have lost sight of the efficacy of their baptism. "In a word, we no longer know whether being baptized is equivalent to being evangelizers," said Archbishop Salvatore Fisichella, president of the Pontifical Council for the Promotion of the New Evangelization, when speaking before the 2012 Synod of Bishops. "Incapable of being proclaimers of the Gospel, unsure of the certainty of the truth that saves, and cautious in speaking because we are oppressed by control of language, we have lost credibility and we risk rendering vain the Pentecost."[3]

We must not receive the sacrament of baptism in vain. We must allow the outpouring of the Holy Spirit in our lives to bear fruit. We must renew our baptismal promises with vigor. From there the "ultimate purpose of mission is to enable people to share in the communion which exists between the Father and the Son."[4]

So if our mission starts with our baptism, where do we go from there? How do we know what to do next?

The implementation of the New Evangelization is sort of like trying to squeeze a banana out of its peel. It can go in a thousand different unexpected directions. So it's helpful to compartmentalize, to an extent, an area of New Evangelization at a time and keeping in mind that your area of focus can change over time. Additionally, you might find yourself focusing on multiple areas of New Evangelization simultaneously.

So what are some of the compartments of New Evangelization in which you may find yourself focusing?

Keep in mind that creating a concise and complete list of areas of New Evangelization is as impossible as categorizing people's favorite foods. (Somewhere out there is a person whose favorite food is chocolate-covered slugs.) I think it's best to think about these categories in buckets, some of which may include:

1. The New Evangelization and You (Yes, you get your own bucket, and I even named this book after your bucket.)

2. The New Evangelization and Home (your spouse, children, and others under your own roof)

3. The New Evangelization and Your Parish (the people you sit next to at Mass, the folks in the choir, and so on)

4. The New Evangelization and Your Diocese (Many people are afraid to take a role on a diocesan level, but there are always events that need volunteers and marketing teams.)

5. The New Evangelization and the World.

Help Wanted: No Experience Necessary

For many years I held positions in the IT industry as a web developer and designer, project and software development manager, and business analyst. In all honesty, though I was very good at my various jobs, I questioned God's logic in placing me in several of them.

For example, in 2000, shortly after accepting a very high-profile and demanding position—overseeing a sizable staff of programmers and coordinating the development of multiple software systems that would be implemented in critically secure financial and banking organizations—I found myself overwhelmed and completely stressed. I was behind on a deadline that required me to document substantially complicated requirements for a financial institution of which I had very little understanding. Knowing that the security of many people's bank accounts was dependent upon the framework of this project, I convinced the director of our division to let me work from home one day, so as to limit my distractions and get the job done.

I ended up with a day of begging God to help me finish this task for which I felt immensely unqualified. After hours of poring over notes from meetings and trying to figure out how to convert those scribbles into documentation that clearly explained to programmers what the banks and our bosses wanted us to build, I was overcome by anxiety and the gravity of the task. I fell prostrate to the ground, put my face in my hands, and screamed.

"God," I prayed, "what are you doing with me? Do you not realize that I was a liberal arts major in college? What am I doing managing the development of software? Why in the world are you entrusting me with something as huge as this project? People could lose their jobs if I don't do this right! Don't you understand, God?"

By the grace of God I persevered, and the project was completed with amazing success. But more than that, I learned a valuable lesson, one that I have applied many times in my faith life.

My experience of leaning heavily on God in my moment of doubt was an opportunity to grow in prudence, "the virtue that disposes practical reason to discern our true good in every circumstance and to choose the right means of achieving it." St. Thomas Aquinas defines prudence as "right reason in action" (*CCC*, 1806, quoting *Summa* II–II, 47, 2).

I am unqualified in just about every initiative I take on in life, especially when it comes to being a New Evangelizer. But God "has qualified us to share in the inheritance of the saints in light" (Colossians 1:12), and he will not leave us to our own devices. He wants us to achieve the goals he places before us.

We all have moments of doubt. We doubt ourselves, we doubt our abilities, and we might even doubt God.

Even the disciples had their moments of doubt. When Jesus appeared to them after the Resurrection, "they were startled and frightened, and supposed that they saw a spirit." Even after Jesus "showed them his hands and feet...they still disbelieved for joy, and wondered" (Luke 24:37–41; see CCC, 644). But God's grace overcomes doubt. Our cooperation with grace leads to the development of virtues, which in turn strengthen our ability to overcome not only doubt but other weaknesses that may inhibit our success as New Evangelizers.

You may not feel qualified to be in the same league as the apostles, but God has called each of us to unity with him, which we receive through our baptism. And through that baptism we are promised, "You shall receive power when the Holy Spirit has come upon you, and you shall be my witnesses…to the end of the earth" (Acts 1:8).

A Little Secret

Lest you still don't believe that God is calling you to something great, allow me to let you in on a little secret about myself.

I mentioned before that I was a liberal arts major. Before that I was an English literature major. And before that I was interested in journalism. I was a terrible student, partially because I was juggling too many things all at once (school, work, social life, and more) but also because I just didn't put in the hard work really necessary to do the job.

In fact (and here's the embarrassing part), I'm not even sure how I got the degree I do possess. No kidding. I'd been in college for several years, fluctuating between full-time and part-time status, changing majors, sometimes accidentally wasting time with classes I didn't need to take, and barely passing other ones I needed to excel at. I honestly lost track of how many credit hours I earned.

One afternoon I heard the doorbell ring, and when I opened the door I saw a postal employee getting back into her vehicle. On the ground next to the door was a flat envelope from the university. Having not had the greatest success in college up to that point, I actually feared that inside the envelope were papers expelling me. Instead, to my absolute amazement and hysterical laughter, inside was a diploma for a degree in liberal arts. I'd graduated from college without even knowing it!

Now, let me ask you a question: Knowing how I got my degree, how do you feel about my writing this book? I don't have a degree in theology (yet), and I don't have a doctorate in Scripture studies (though perhaps someday I will). Does that make me unqualified to share the faith?

God doesn't take the qualified and make them worthy. He takes the unworthy and makes them qualified.

When it comes to being a New Evangelizer and knowing the faith more deeply, living the faith more fully, and sharing the faith more successfully, God doesn't look at the degrees and accomplishments on your resume. He looks at your earnestness to serve him, the love you're willing to express to others through your actions, and your willingness to allow the Holy Spirit to work through you, an unworthy servant. God isn't just looking for people with a wall full of diplomas (though he'll gladly use them too). God is more interested in applicants who want to get busy working for his kingdom.

When my wife and I got engaged, my only job was playing guitar and singing (badly) for lattes and tips in a coffeehouse in downtown Atlanta. I had no real job, no real prospects, no real training, and no real future. But look at some of the things God has allowed me to do, none of which I had ever imagined:

- created, wrote, and starred in a sitcom pilot with our good friends Mac and Katherine Barron (the hosts of the *Catholic in a Small Town* podcast) for The CatholicTV Network (which you can watch, by the way, at http://massconfusion-sitcom.com)
- hosted a three-hour-a-day Catholic talk show on international satellite radio for several years

- created award-winning media productions that have been downloaded over five million times
- cowrote and published a book with my wife
- spoke before tens of thousands of people on various aspects of Catholicism
- launched a video series about the Catholic faith that is now used in homes and parishes around the world (www. ThatCatholicShow.com)
- won multiple awards for television and audio productions
- was named a leader in Catholic New Media by the Franciscan University of Steubenville
- interviewed countless cardinals and bishops, along with secular celebrities like Kevin Bacon, Julie Andrews, Neil Sedaka, Dion, Nathan Fillion, Sean Astin, and many more.

I don't point all this out to brag but rather to emphasize that if God can do all of these things through an idiot like me, imagine how valuable *you* are to him. Here's the sincere truth, and I say this at the risk of sounding like a preacher promising the Prosperity Gospel: God can take *you* down unexpected paths, into amazing adventures, and more deeply into your faith if you're open to it and his will allows. Yes, I know, that sounds like a cliché. But the only way my wife and I have accomplished anything is simply by the grace of God.

Would I like to have a better education? Absolutely, and I'm actively working on that goal. And if the chancellor of some Catholic university is reading this and wants to give me an honorary doctorate, I'll gladly accept it (hint, hint, hint). But ultimately that doesn't matter. What matters is that now that I've fallen in love with my faith and have grown closer to God than I could have ever imagined, I'm just honored to be put to work in the fields of the Lord.

I'm not "worthy" to write the book that you're reading. The fact that I was given the opportunity to do so—to encourage you to take gradual steps in knowing, living, and sharing your faith—only shows that God can take any of us and put us to work.

Maybe you're like me and don't have a degree (yet) that you're really proud of. So what? Neither did Jesus.

Questions

1. How would you answer the question, "Why are you Catholic?"

2. Has there been a time in your life when you felt unqualified for a job or task? How did God help you through that?

3. What are some ways (think big!) that you would like to serve God, even if those ways seem impossible to achieve on your own?

Prayer for New Evangelizers

Lord,

it is my hope to serve you.

Please send your Holy Spirit to increase my knowledge

of you,

to help me better grasp your Word,

and clearly see the direction you want me to take in the

New Evangelization,

that I might find my way to you

and be a witness to others along the way.

Amen.

chapter eight

Becoming a New Evangelizer

> Mistakes are the usual bridge between inexperience
> and wisdom.
> —PHYLLIS THEROUX[1]

In his apostolic letter At the Beginning of the Third Millennium, Pope John Paul II wrote, "We must revive in ourselves the burning conviction of Paul, who cried out: 'Woe to me if I do not preach the gospel' (1 Corinthians 9:16)."[2]

Quoting Vatican II, the *Catechism of the Catholic Church* states that we "'must profess before men the faith they have received from God through the Church' and participate in the apostolic and missionary activity of the People of God" (CCC, 1270, quoting *Lumen Gentium*, 11; see *Lumen Gentium*, 17; *Ad gentes*, 7, 23).

If we are going to evangelize, we need to know what it is, exactly, that we are evangelizing. The answer to that question has multiple parts, but the first answer can be found each morning when you look in the mirror. The New Evangelization begins with your being re-evangelized.

Stop Chugging

There was a program on television a few years back called *God or the Girl*. The premise of this reality show was to follow several young Catholic men over the course of some weeks as each discerned God's purpose in their lives: priesthood or marriage. All of them were on fire for God and were willing to go to extremes to prove their love. One went to a foreign country to work as a missionary. Another broke up with his girlfriend, thinking he was headed for the seminary. And yet another carried a heavy wooden cross a long distance in emulation of Jesus Christ.

I'll never forget one scene in which the cross-bearing guy was engaged in a scriptural debate with a Protestant. Though he had a fierce love for God and was willing to do absolutely anything for Christ, when it came to bantering Scripture with a much more studied adversary (not that our Protestant brothers and sisters should be considered adversaries), he was absolutely trumped. I could relate to that far too well.

When I first started taking my Catholic faith more seriously as an adult, I had a terrible time memorizing Bible verses, let alone remembering paragraphs out of the *Catechism*. And it's not just because of the subject matter. I've always had difficulty memorizing stuff.

In sixth grade I had to memorize every single preposition in the English language, and our test in school was simply to take out a piece of paper and write them all down. Trying to take in that whole list all at once brought me to tears. My brain just couldn't hold it all in. In high school and college, Spanish classes were the bane of my existence, simply because I couldn't process the endless forms of different words.

Granted, I didn't really care about prepositions. And I never really expected to use Spanish, so my desire was never really there either. If I'd known that I would eventually marry a woman whose parents are native Spanish speakers from Puerto Rico, I probably would have been more motivated.

But I *want* to know about my faith, and I *want* to be able to explain it. I *want* to be able to quote Scripture, chapter and verse. I *want* to "always be prepared to make a defense to any one to account for the hope that is in [me]" (1 Peter 3:15).

Yet I found myself regularly cowering behind my ignorance. "I'm not an apologist, and I can't memorize Scripture, but..." Then I'd stumble about and attempt to give at least a halfhearted explanation of my faith. Rarely did I find success in my attempts to share the faith with others.

Over the years I tired of excuses. I *wanted* to be an apologist and defender of our faith in a world that seems completely oblivious to the beauty and joy of Catholicism. I eventually accepted the fact that, though I'll never know the entirety of the Catholic faith, I am more than capable of retaining the basics and sharing them with others.

So don't give up.

For new Catholics, or for cradle Catholics like me who never took the faith seriously until they were adults, attempting to take in the fullness and richness of the Catholic Church is somewhat like trying to take a drink from a fire hose. We have such a rich history of both Scripture and Tradition, through the guidance of the Holy Spirit and the teaching authority of the pope and the magisterium, that taking it all in at once would blast you out of your seat. That was my situation, anyway, in trying to imagine myself as one who could confidently master the teachings of the Church and wisdom of Scripture.

What worked for me was taking small sips, rather than trying to chug everything at once. I began to simply focus on small bits of information at a time. Rather than learning a verse of Scripture a day, I'd give myself a week or even a month to commit one to memory. Rather than feeling the need to read St. Thomas Aquinas's *Summa Theologica* in a week, I read the *Catechism of the Catholic Church* over the period of a year.

In other words, rather than trying to force God into my brain, I allowed him to penetrate my life at the pace he made me capable of.

By the way, I intentionally ended that last sentence with a preposition, just to show that I know that one. It is possible to learn difficult lessons. And more times than not, the hard lessons learned are the ones we'll long remember.

New Evangelizers in Action: Jason Morrow and the Penance Project

In late 2010 Jason Morrow started an apostolate called "The Penance Project." Its mission is to promote the sacrament of penance, through which God provides forgiveness and grace to those who seek it.

"For those who send in a request, I mail them back a 'Penance Kit,'" Jason explains. "In the kit is an information packet with laminated pages that describe the sacrament, an examination of conscience of their choice (adult, teen, child), instructions on how to go to confession, and common prayers that they can refer to."

In addition to mailing the content to people who request it, all of the information is also available on the website for the Penance Project, www.thepenanceproject.org. Currently Jason is working on how to promote the Penance Project through social media.

THE NEW EVANGELIZATION AND YOU

As a convert, one of the biggest challenges Jason has encountered in knowing the faith is simply avoiding erroneous information.

"On many occasions those who were teaching me about the faith left out or twisted the full truth, so on many important aspects of Church teaching, I was confused, I misunderstood, or I was ignorant," says Jason. "In some ways it was a blessing, because it was through those inconsistencies that I encountered among other Catholics that I began to search out the truth for myself and scrutinize why the Church taught it."

Looking to the future of the Church and the New Evangelization, Jason says, "My hope is that we all are strengthened in our continual conversion and that we more boldly live out the gospel in our day-to-day lives, and that by living out the gospel life we inspire and attract everyone to Christ."

Ongoing Relationships

Ultimately, the New Evangelization is about knowing Jesus and helping others to do the same. As discussed in the previous chapter, Jesus left us the Catholic Church as an instrument to lead us closer to him through the sacramental life it offers. Yet even if you are a daily communicant, there is still more to know about Jesus Christ.

If you already know him, the New Evangelization is about knowing him better. Again, even if you're the pope, you can know Jesus better.

Now, that knowing is not some sort of achievement or goal or checklist of objectives, so that one day you can proudly say, "I got all of my Jesus boxes checked! I know Jesus!" Our relationship with Jesus Christ—our personal relationship—should be one of constant conversion, evaluation, and growth.

When my wife, Jennifer, and I got married back in 1995, I barely knew her. Of course, at the time I thought I knew everything there was to know. But now we've been married long enough that I know my wife far, far better—but probably not as well as my dad knows my mom, for my parents have been married nearly six decades.

Jennifer and I—through trials and joys and children and new coats of paint and diets and broken bones (not that we've broken each other's bones!)—have grown closer together and more in love than we ever imagined possible on the day of our wedding. It's probably safe to say that by the time one of us leaves this earthly plane, I'll know her far better than I do today.

That's because our relationship is not just about that day that we claimed each other as husband and wife, when we gave ourselves to each other and committed our lives to each other completely. Our relationship is about every day and every event that's happened since and will ever happen until the days we draw our last breaths. And even then we probably won't know everything there is to know about each other.

Jesus Christ is the Bridegroom, and we, the body of Christ, are his bride. It's fair to suggest that we will never know Jesus 100 percent in this life. Having a relationship with Christ is not just a matter of giving ourselves and our lives to him one day: "I commit my life to you, Jesus. We good?" We can't assume that that is all there is to it and then move about our merry way, expecting to have a great relationship with Christ. That would be like my committing my life to my wife back in 1995, saying, "We good? See you in heaven," and then going off and living a life independent of her, never taking the time to continually nurture and grow in that relationship.

Though we may have accepted Jesus Christ on one memorable day, our relationship is not about that day. Our friendship, our relationship, our ongoing commitment to Jesus Christ, needs to be one of constant exploration and discovery. The guidance of the Holy Spirit should draw us into closer union with Christ and with his entire holy Church.

Your life might be moving at a thousand miles an hour—between work and family and friends and school and whatever else might fill the time between sunrise and lights out. But in the midst of all that busyness is a stationary God waiting for you to rotate your life around him.

We're not in the Dark Ages. Let's not subscribe to some wacko belief that the Son should revolve around us instead of us around the Son.

Describing Jesus

How would you describe Jesus Christ and your relationship to him? What is it about your personal encounters and experiences with Christ that would make yours a compelling witness to others in this world?

Going back to the example of my relationship with my wife, I would also say that there are countless ways she has made me a better man. Jennifer has caused me to trust God more, to lean on God more. She has given me great examples of patience with our children, which I sometimes struggle to emulate.

If you've ever listened to any of our radio shows or podcasts, you'll know that Jennifer is the eternal optimist, the glass-half-full kind of person. I'm typically the person who knocks over the glass, spills all the milk, and then shatters the glass on the floor just for good measure. I'm constantly trying to figure out how to be more upbeat, like Jennifer. And in the years we've been married, she has helped me improve tremendously in that area.

Who in your life has prodded you to be better than you would be on your own? Perhaps it was a sibling, coworker, spouse, parent, or friend. Now think about how you would describe that person to someone else. What part of your life has been changed for the better as a result of that person?

Now, in the way that you describe someone else who is near and dear to you, how would you describe Jesus Christ?

Perhaps the best way to tell others about Jesus is by the witness of your own behavior. People who know you well can see how being closer to Jesus has made you a better, more fulfilled, and more enriched person.

> You are the light of the world.... Let your light so shine before men, that they may see your good works and give glory to your Father who is in heaven. (Matthew 5:14, 16)

Don't be fooled. If you are the light of the world, that light didn't come from your own greatness. It came from God, who has called you to sainthood.

Questions

1. How would you describe Jesus Christ if someone asked you who he is?

2. What is the best way for you to learn new things? Do you need lots of repetition? Do you learn best by hearing something explained or by seeing it on paper?

3. Imagine how you would like your relationship with Jesus to be one month from now. What concrete actions can you take to make that happen? (See chapter ten for ideas if you need them.)

Prayer for Open Eyes

Lord,

please help me to have open eyes each day—

eyes to see you in the world,

eyes to see you in others,

eyes to see you in my family and friends,

eyes to see you in my enemies,

eyes to see you in myself,

eyes to see you working in me and through me,

eyes to see you in the challenges of my day,

eyes to see you in moments of peace,

eyes to see you in moments of joy,

and eyes to see opportunities to introduce you to those I

encounter today and always.

Amen.

chapter nine

Twenty-First–Century Fishing Tips

> And were we to enter into a more detailed investiga-
> tion of these matters, an endless number of endless
> questions would arise, which would involve us in a
> larger work than the present occasion admits. We
> cannot be expected to find room for replying to every
> question that may be started by unoccupied and
> captious men, who are ever more ready to ask ques-
> tions than capable of understanding the answer.
> —St. Augustine, *City of God*, Book 15

I have a brother who is, by every definition, an outdoorsman.
I've often said that if there was ever some cataclysmic event in
which all the power sources crashed and the world was sent into
anarchy, I'd be loading my family in the van and making a beeline
for my brother's house. That's one sure way I'd be able to feed my
children.

My brother has hunted, fished, and built things with his hands
since we were kids. He can clean a mess of fish like nobody's business. With a cooler of freshly caught fish and a carving knife, he
is a sight to behold.

Every spring my brother calls me on the phone to let me know
when the "striper" first begin to swell to the surface as the weather

warms and spawning season nears. Though I've yet to witness it, my brother and his friends claim that at that time of the year, there are a few special days when the striped bass swarm with such intensity that you can't put your fishing line into the water without bringing up a fish. Even my dad has claimed to witness this, though I still suspect the photographs are just well-done Photoshop mockups.

I always arrive for a fishing expedition having somehow forgotten the various challenges that have accompanied our previous outings on the water. In my mind fishing is supposed to be as simple as driving to a lake, climbing into a boat, casting a line, and *Bam!*, there's your fish. Instead, fishing includes driving three hours to my brother's house, loading the boat with gear, realizing I need a temporary out-of-state fishing license, going to the store, filling out paperwork, getting the license, going to the grocery story, buying provisions, going back to my brother's house, hooking the boat to the truck, going to the gas station, getting gas for the boat, finally getting to the river, loading the boat into the river, cruising about two miles upstream, and finally casting a line.

And then waiting.

And casting again.

And then waiting.

Some days, after much pleading to St. Peter, St. Andrew, and any other saints who once made a living chasing fish, I might actually feel that excitement of a hit on the line, the thrill of jerking the rod back and sinking the hook, the thrust of the rod's handle into my gut, and such a monumental battle that it leaves a tender purple bruise on my abdomen.

All of this effort may seem excessive but for the blessing of being out on the slick surface of a river at sunset or sunrise and brought closer to God simply because of the experience. And I have on occasion caught some amazingly huge fish (honest!).

It may seem like a stretch, but I believe that all the work that goes into fishing is one of the reasons why the activity is featured so highly in Scripture. We know that when Jesus told Peter and Andrew, "Follow me, and I will make you fishers of men" (Matthew 4:19), that call would not always be simple. Seeking people and the conversion of souls seems like (and is) a worthy endeavor, but it's never as simple as we might hope.

Fishing requires knowledge, patience, and perseverance. Some days you come home empty-handed. Some days all you catch are small fish. Other days you find yourself confronted with a legendary beast that tests your mettle and every ounce of your ability. But if you ask a fisherman, every fish is worth catching, and every trip onto the water is worth the effort.

And if you ask a Christian committed to serving God and devoted to offering each day up to him, every day in the service of God is worthwhile. Every time we cast out our nets, seeking the conversion of souls for the glory of God, God uses our effort, if only to develop our humility, our patience, or some other valuable virtue. And when a soul is indeed caught in the love of Christ and turns back to him, the reward is priceless. For we know that "there will be more joy in heaven over one sinner who repents than over ninety-nine righteous persons who need no repentance" (Luke 15:7).

New Evangelizers in Action: Aaron Kelly—Teenage Catechist

Aaron Kelly is a seventeen-year-old high school student who teaches junior high religious education at his parish in the diocese of Rochester. He tries to place the New Evangelization at the heart of his lessons.

"For example," Aaron explains, "I have the students at the end of each class turn on their cell phones and make a Facebook post, or send a text message to a friend, about what we learned that day. One day we talked about vocations, and I had them text, 'What does God want you to do with your life?'"

As a teenager himself, Aaron says that "finding resources that are youth-friendly to explain the questions I have or questions people ask me about the faith" is one of the biggest challenges he has in getting to know the faith better. Some books geared toward youth that are helpful and entertaining are Mark Hart's *Blessed Are the Bored in Spirit* (Servant, 2006) and *Ask the Bible Geek,* volumes 1 and 2 (Servant, 2003, 2007). The latter two have a reader-friendly question-and-answer format.

Aaron hopes that the New Evangelization will bring about a greater respect and understanding of the sacraments. "I hope that Catholics will strengthen their faith in the real presence of Jesus Christ in the Eucharist, as statistics show that most Catholics don't even believe in the real presence. If we have faith in the real presence and receive the Eucharist weekly, we can have faith in all things."

From that Communion with Christ, Aaron says, "I hope, and this is my task, to set a fire in the hearts of my peers, young people my age, to live their faith in their daily life and not be afraid to share the gospel."

Catch the Easiest Fish First

If fishing requires a certain unexpected level of preparation for even a modicum of success, an even greater level of preparation is necessary in the New Evangelization, in which we try to catch souls for Christ. The difference is that with fishing, if you don't have bait, there's no point in even trying. But when sharing our faith with others, we have a responsibility to be witnesses, to share our faith, to engage the culture and draw others to Christ, even if we feel completely unprepared and unqualified.

Going back to chapter one, many Christians fail to evangelize simply because they're afraid. They think they're not smart enough. They think they're not ready to go after big fish, so they don't go after any fish at all.

One of the keys to the New Evangelization is that, while the "big fish" are nice, there are a lot of smaller fish just waiting to be brought into the boat.

What do I mean by "big fish"? If the guy in the cube next to you thinks that Catholics worship an imaginary creature in the sky and eat crackers that they say are actually the body of someone they worship, you might want to skip trying to invite him to Mass until you've had more time (maybe even years) to grow in your own understanding of the faith and put that faith into practice more fully. He's what I'd call a big fish—someone who is going to need a lot of convincing.

We oftentimes get caught up with converting all the atheists and non-Christians we know, but what about the small fish in your life? In the New Evangelization, that's one of the most important questions you can ask.

What about inviting those around you to church, those who perhaps have allowed the business of life to take priority but who would be open to hearing about the joy you experience in having Jesus Christ in your life?

What about your friends and family who have no problem with Jesus but don't know how to make him the center of their lives?

These are the small fish, the easier catches. And they're no less important than the big fish. Each of us is a child of God. God doesn't care if we catch Moby Dick or a tiny minnow. He just wants us to catch fish for him. He welcomes them all, including the smallest and easiest catches.

Think about it. If you have limited time and resources each day—among family, work, and other responsibilities—and if you feel like an amateur fisher rather than an experienced angler, focus on the catchable fish all around the boat. Meanwhile you will build up your ability to go after the great white sharks in your life.

A Fish Named Bill

It may seem wrong to flat-out ignore someone who doesn't know Jesus or even believe in God. Watching someone turn his back on his Creator is a terrible thing to witness. But some people have absolutely no desire to do anything different.

For example, during the writing of this book I received an e-mail from a man named Bill, a sixty-five-year-old self-identified former Catholic who frequently listened to my radio show, *The Catholics Next Door*. Bill listened to our show each week, not because he agreed with me on the tenets of Catholicism but because he wanted to garner an understanding of the mind-set of Catholics who actually agree with the teachings of the Catholic Church.

Bill fits the description of many fallen-away Catholics:

I attended Catholic schools for twelve years, was an altar boy, and memorized the entire Mass in Latin. I would follow the missal in Latin and look for aspects of grammar as it flowed. I was in high school at the height of Vatican II and identified with the Church role in social justice.... During my university years I inquired into alternative views upon our curious appearance on this planet. I read Bertrand Russell, the stoic philosophers, particularly Epictetus, and roots of dissent appearing in the Enlightenment. I also read such works as the *Tao* by Lao Tzu; I read about Buddhist philosophies, world mythologies, and other perspectives inconsistent with Catholic dogma. So many touchstones pointing to our common humanity and spirit.

Bill is obviously intelligent and desirous of higher learning, but from an early age he identified Catholicism as something restrictive instead of freeing, something oppressive instead of loving. When I asked him about his impressions of the Catholic Church today, Bill wrote that "it is an institution that assigns every contrary position on the 'sanctity of life' to the darkest corner possible, one where no contrary voice is permitted."

This statement, in particular, made me very sad. As one who regularly speaks with people in the pro-life movement, I know the incredible good they do in giving voice to the voiceless—indeed, helping all human life from the moment of conception to the moment of natural death. And here's someone who looks at the Catholic Church's life-giving message as a strangulation of opposing viewpoints.

Bill went on,

Historical evidence clearly reveals that the primacy of Peter [as] first pope is more than slightly delusional, yet it remains [the Church's] keystone belief. All historical evidence indicates that Peter was present to the east of Jerusalem, but it is quite thoroughly known that he was never in Rome. The keys, the throne, and all so-called bases for this evidence are all relics of the Roman Empire.

In Bill's responses, there are many inaccuracies about what the Catholic Church teaches and what she has done. There are also severe overgeneralizations, such as, "*All* historical evidence indicates…" We know that's not true simply because of the historical evidence of two thousand years of Catholic Church teaching.

Should I have answered each of Bill's points, taking the time to do significant research to craft appropriate rebuttals? He is a child of God, after all, deserving of love and respect. God loves Bill as much as he loves you and me. So don't I owe it to God to spend as much time as necessary helping Bill see that God loves him?

It may sound harsh, but I feel the answer is no.

Bill would be considered a big fish. He has strong opinions and decades of experiences and gathered knowledge that frame his negative outlook of Catholicism and most other "organized" religions. And I suspect he would ignore the most well-researched and carefully worded responses.

That may sound incredibly negative, but it's not. It's a realistic perspective.

Would I want Bill to experience the joy and love of a relationship with Jesus Christ within the Catholic Church? Absolutely. Do I think that many of his views and opinions are incorrect and that thorough answers and responses are available from countless sources? Certainly. But some people aren't really looking for answers. That's a sad, sad reality.

Now, I didn't shut Bill out. In fact, I sent him follow-up questions and expressed genuine interest in why he left the Church. I told him that I appreciated his time and his honesty as well. But the reality is that there is very little else I could do to convince Bill. To continue a pursuit of this big fish would be a disservice to the ocean of fish desperate to be reeled in, those the Holy Spirit is calling me to befriend, who are more open to what Jesus Christ wants to do in their lives.

Is it wrong to ignore these people? Well, don't ignore them outright. These people need our love and understanding. If Bill was your friend or a family member, I'd encourage you to continue loving him, talking with him, and praying for him. Just remember that his conversion will not be accomplished by you. It will be done through the Holy Spirit, who may choose to act *through* you. But don't get discouraged about your evangelizing potential if you don't witness Bill's conversion.

If you know and care for a big fish and are willing to invest a significant amount of your time and passion to work through an endless barrage of questions in the hope that the Holy Spirit will touch that person's heart, go for it! But keep in mind that some people have no desire to be converted. Honestly, the best thing you can do for them is pray.

Pray a lot. Offer up Masses and rosaries and sacrifices. And remember in the end that Jesus leads people through the often-times treacherous waters of this life. That doesn't let you off the hook (to mix my fishing metaphors), but it should give you some focus.

Once at my grandfather's lake house, I discovered that if I just dropped a line with a hook into the water, some tiny fish would swim right up and jump on the line—without any bait at all!

What little fish are in your life? Who do you know who hasn't been to church in a while but might appreciate an invitation? Sometimes it takes very little to get a fish on the line.

Operation Andrew

Remember the Billy Graham Crusade training I attended at a Catholic parish years ago, the one that simultaneously made me doubt my Catholic faith and then somehow catapulted me into a greater love and understanding of Catholicism than ever before? One of the most positive aspects of that training was an interesting experiment called "Operation Andrew."

The idea was based on John 1:35–42. John the Baptist was with two of his disciples, when he saw Jesus and called out, "Behold, the Lamb of God!" At that point the two disciples went after Jesus, who then invited them to accompany him. One of these two was St. Andrew, the brother of Simon.

The first thing Andrew did after seeing Jesus was to go to his brother and tell him, "We have found the Messiah." He brought Simon to Jesus, who gave Simon the new name Cephas, which means "Peter." Yes, this was the first pope! Later Jesus would say to Peter:

> I tell you, you are Peter, and on this rock I will build my Church, and the gates of Hades shall not prevail against it. I will give you the keys of the kingdom of heaven, and whatever you bind on earth shall be bound in heaven, and whatever you loose on earth shall be loosed in heaven. (Matthew 16:18–19)

You could say that this was one of the first examples of *primary evangelization*, of introducing someone to Jesus Christ. The goal of Operation Andrew, then, was to encourage all Christians to exhibit the enthusiasm of St. Andrew in inviting others to an encounter with Jesus.

Have you ever eaten in a fancy restaurant and ordered a dessert that made your eyes roll up into your brain, it tasted so good? Your taste buds did a tango, and it was all you could do to eat slowly and not down the whole delicacy in one enormous gulp? And if you were dining with someone else, what did you do? Most likely you said, "Oh my, you have *got* to taste this!"

Maybe you've done that with a song: "You have *got* to hear this." Or a video of a chimpanzee riding on a Segway that you've seen online: "You have *got* to see this."

When we experience something amazing in life, the desire to share it with others wells up within us. That desire to pass on an extremely positive experience borders on a need. It bubbles up within us and practically gushes out of us.

That's how it must have been for St. Andrew. He had just discovered the *promised Savior of the world!* He couldn't contain that. He couldn't keep it to himself. The experience he'd just witnessed—"Behold, the Lamb of God!"—was so absolutely mind-blowing that he couldn't keep it in.

The Operation Andrew exercise I participated in tapped into that need to share the greatest gift of all time—Jesus Christ—with other people in my life. The challenge, however, was doing it in such a way that I wouldn't freak somebody out. I didn't want to come off like a "Jesus freak," only interested in a conversion quota rather than in the life of someone else.

As a part of this project, each parishioner was given a card and encouraged to make a list of people they knew who currently did not have a relationship with Jesus Christ. Then we made a commitment to pray for those people on a daily basis. When I got my card, first I brainstormed and made a list of coworkers, neighbors, and relatives. To keep the project manageable and to ensure that I'd actually pray for people on a regular basis, I narrowed the list down to about five or six names.

So what did I pray for? First and foremost, I prayed that God would become a part of these people's lives. I asked that God would open each of their hearts to a greater understanding of Jesus's desire to be the center of their daily existence and to offer them forgiveness for sins. Additionally, I prayed that the Holy Spirit would somehow give me opportunities to witness on his behalf, despite how ill-prepared I might have been to answer any questions. The eventual goal was to find opportunities to invite those on my list to church or to some other event where they might encounter Jesus Christ.

What's interesting is that through this experience I began to deepen my understanding of Catholicism. I was praying for others on my Operation Andrew list, but I needed to be reintroduced to Jesus Christ just as much as they did. I was asking what seemed like a thousand questions a day about my faith. Unable to find answers from those I asked, I ended up reading several books during that time, each of which had a dramatic effect on my faith while simultaneously increasing my knowledge of Catholicism.

For the record, I'll never forget three books and one audio presentation that somehow (most likely providentially) came my way during that time of questioning. The books were *Rome Sweet*

Home by Scott and Kimberly Hahn; *One, Holy, Catholic, and Apostolic* by Kenneth Whitehead; and *Triumph: The Power and Glory of the Catholic Church* by H.W. Crocker III. The audio presentation was a talk by Dr. Janet Smith called *Contraception: Why Not?* These resources gave me a better understanding of the Catholic faith.

So in my efforts to bring others closer to Jesus, I was drawn into a deeper understanding and relationship with him and the Catholic faith. And of the people I listed all those years ago, one former atheist joined the Catholic Church within two years, and a Catholic who had been as wishy-washy as I was started praying the rosary and attending daily Mass.

Who are the people you'd put on your Operation Andrew list? Write those down and make a commitment to simply pray for them each day. At the top of that list, I'd recommend you put your own name. Pray to be reminded on a regular basis of the ways that Jesus has impacted your life.

Prayer for others and for ourselves is the first step in the New Evangelization. Sometimes that's *all* we have to do; God will do the rest.

Questions

1. Do you know anyone (maybe you) who went through a conversion experience? How did the prayers of others affect that conversion?

2. What are some of the most common objections you hear people give to the Catholic Church? What are some possible ways to respond to those objections?

3. Who would you put on your "Operation Andrew" list?

Prayer for Sharing

Lord,

I am a humble fisher who on my own can catch no one for you.

But I ask you for the grace to be a witness on your behalf. I ask for the opportunity to see the conversions of my family and friends.

Lead those I love into your loving arms,

and if it is your will, allow me to be part of that.

Amen.

chapter ten

A Year of New Evangelizing

> Go therefore and make disciples of all nations,
> baptizing them in the name of the Father and of the
> Son and of the Holy Spirit, teaching them to observe
> all that I have commanded you.
> —MATTHEW 28:19–20

I hope by now you've started thinking of different ways in which you can play a vital role in the New Evangelization—in knowing, living, and sharing your Catholic faith in this world. While it would be impossible to develop a set of hard-and-fast rules for how to do one or all of those things, there are definitely parameters that you can set up to help you be more successful.

Throughout this book I've challenged you to think of large and small ways of knowing, living, and sharing your faith. I've encouraged you to set daily, weekly, monthly, and yearly goals for developing a greater spirituality and closeness with God. But even with all this encouragement, sometimes finding a tangible thing to do on a regular basis is as hard as figuring out what to make for dinner on a Monday night when you forgot to buy groceries over the weekend. Not that we've ever done that in our house, of course.

Below are three lists with a full year's worth of ideas for knowing your faith, living your faith, and sharing your faith. I love brainstorming. My thought is that I'd rather come up with a hundred ideas just to find one great one instead of coming up with just one idea that may or may not work for everyone.

The way you use these lists is completely up to you. Some of you might be inspired to follow them chronologically throughout the year, taking an item from each list each week. This is fine, but don't allow yourself to become discouraged if you take on a challenge and fail miserably. Also, don't think that once you do something on the list, you must continue to do it every week. This is not meant to be a cumulative to-do list resulting in hundreds of new responsibilities by the end of the year.

You might look at these lists to get you moving in the right direction if you ever find yourself struggling to move forward in your faith. When your faith is feeling dry and stale, it can be good to challenge yourself with an activity that forces you outside of your comfort zone. Too often in life I get bored with a routine and need to shake things up. If that happens to you, I hope these lists of ideas will help.

If one choice seems too easy or too difficult, pick a different one. Or perhaps you'll find one suggestion so beneficial that you'll choose to do it over and over again for a whole year, sort of like your own Catholic version of *Groundhog Day* with Bill Murray.

As you pray over these ideas, ask the Holy Spirit to inspire you to put some of them into action. Or maybe he'll help you come up with more ways to know, live, and share the faith in your particular circumstances.

New Evangelizers in Action: Suzanne Haugh and Goodness Reigns

"There is a lot to know about being Catholic, and I am behind, trying to catch up!" says Suzanne Haugh, executive director of Goodness Reigns, a nonprofit organization whose mission is to engage and empower people (primarily teens and young adults) to create faith-based media and art.

"While I attended Catholic schools for most of my elementary and high school years, I wish I had grown up learning more of the meat, the *why,* of Church teachings," Suzanne says. "There have been a lot of positive changes since Vatican II. However, I think…the faith… when I was young was often watered down or not explained well."

Suzanne founded Goodness Reigns to help others see the richness of Catholicism through videos.

"On my part there is a desire to attract people to explore the Catholic faith," Suzanne says. "Walls can go up immediately when contrasting views are expressed in conversations. However, with a video—a well-done video—points often can be made that wouldn't have occurred in a conversation because of our walls."

But not everyone is called to make videos, right?

"We believe everyone can create a video that can speak to someone, but they may not have the skills to do so at first," says Suzanne. "This is why we offer the online Goodness Reigns Film School. Gabriel Castillo is the host of short how-to videos that cover…lighting, sound, composition, and other topics necessary for creating a short video that communicates effectively and also inspires viewers."

Evidence of the reach of Goodness Reigns can be seen in the listing of those who entered its first contest for World Youth Day. There were over sixty-six submissions from over thirty-five dioceses in twenty-three states, as well as some from India, Mexico, Canada, and Pakistan.

You can learn more about Suzanne's efforts in New Evangelization at www.GoodnessReigns.com.

Fifty-Two Ways to Know Your Faith

1. Pick one book of the Bible and read it all the way through at least once. Start with a short book, such as James or the Gospel of Mark.

2. Read John chapter 6.

3. Use the index of citations in the back of the *Catechism* to see what the Church teaches about the daily Mass readings this week.

4. Find out what sixteen documents came from Vatican II.

5. Read paragraphs 1420–1498 in the *Catechism of the Catholic Church* about the sacrament of penance.

6. Read *Humanae Vitae* (Encyclical Letter on the Regulation of Birth, available at www.vatican.va) by Pope Pius VI.

7. Watch an episode (or all of them) of *That Catholic Show* at www.ThatCatholicShow.com.

8. Read any of the awesome Catholic historical novels by Louis de Wohl, which will give you a greater appreciation for various saints.

9. Find a local Catholic radio station or satellite channel, and listen to it when you're in your car.

10. Visit a Catholic bookstore. Ask God to point out a book he may want you to read.

11. Search for "Catholic" in iTunes, and download some Catholic podcasts. (NewEvangelizers.com has several titles, including *The Catholics Next Door.*)

12. Go listen to a Catholic speaker.

13. Read any one of the sixteen documents from Vatican II.

14. Go to Zenit.org and read news about the Catholic Church every day. You can subscribe to Zenit's e-newsletter and automatically receive it in your inbox each day.

15. Find the Scripture passages that correspond with the mysteries of the rosary, and underline them or mark them in your Bible, "First Joyful Mystery," "Second Joyful Mystery," and so on. (There is a full list of these Scripture passages at www.RosaryArmy.com.)

16. Choose a book to help you read the Bible. I highly recommend *Walking With God: A Journey Through the Bible* by Tim Grey and Jeff Cavins (Ascension, 2010), as well as *Bible Basics for Catholics: A New Picture of Salvation History* by John Bergsma (Ave Maria, 2012).

17. Get a copy of the classic *Life of Christ* by Venerable Fulton J. Sheen. Read just one chapter this week and ponder it.

18. Find a book on Church history, and marvel at the fact that Catholicism has been around for over two thousand years. I highly recommend *Triumph: The Power and the Glory of the Catholic Church* by H.W. Crocker III and *The History of the Church* (The Didache Series) by Fr. Peter Armenio.

19. Subscribe to Catholic magazines and newspapers—and read them.

20. Attend Theology on Tap, a Eucharistic Congress, or a Catholic conference. If one of these events isn't happening in your area any time soon, plan ahead to make sure you won't miss it when one does.

21. Learn how to pray the Chaplet of Divine Mercy. (Ewtn.com has a page on this.)

22. Learn about total consecration to Jesus through Mary at www.TotalConsecration.com.

23. Make an investment: Get Fr. Robert Barron's *Catholicism* DVD series and watch it.

24. Purchase and read a chapter from *Catholicism for Dummies* by Fr. John Trigilio Jr. and Fr. Kenneth Brighenti. Awesome book.

25. Buy the annual Catholic Almanac from Our Sunday Visitor, and be amazed.

26. Buy tabs for your *Catechism* (available from the Coming Home Network), install them, and use them.

27. Memorize the *Memorare* and pray it regularly:

Remember, O most gracious Virgin Mary,

that never was it known

that anyone who fled to thy protection,

implored thy help,

or sought thy intercession was left unaided.

Inspired by this confidence I fly unto thee,

O Virgin of virgins, my mother.

To thee do I come; before thee I stand,

sinful and sorrowful.

O Mother of the Word Incarnate,

despise not my petitions,

but in thy mercy, hear and answer me. Amen.

28. Watch Catholic television. Both EWTN and The CatholicTV Network are available on cable, satellite, the Internet, and ROKU boxes.

29. Download and read (from www.vatican.va) Pope Benedict

XVI's first encyclical letter, *Deus Caritas Est.*

30. Get a *Compendium of the Catechism of the Catholic Church.* Read and pray about one question each day.

31. Pick one line of Scripture, memorize it chapter and verse, and practice it throughout the week.

32. Read Pope John Paul II's Apostolic Letter on the Rosary, *Rosarium Virginis Mariae,* by which he added the luminous mysteries of the rosary and provided insight to praying the rosary in the modern world.

33. Brush up on the Ten Commandments, starting with the *Catechism,* paragraphs 2052–2082.

34. Learn how to use RSS (Really Simple Syndication) feeds and start subscribing to (and reading) Catholic blogs and news services. (Google Reader is a good place to subscribe.) Subscribing is free and will give you access to all of the blog and news content you want in one place. Start by subscribing to the New Evangelizers blog at http://newevangelizers.com/feed.

35. Find out about the patron saint of your home parish. You can find information at catholic-forum.com/saints or in the *Catholic Encyclopedia* at newadvent.org.

36. Take time to read the section about baptism in the *Catechism,* and ponder the importance of your own baptism and your call to discipleship in today's world. If you were baptized as an infant, perhaps there's something new to learn about this important sacrament that continues to affect each of us throughout our lives.

37. Read *Dei Verbum* (Dogmatic Constitution on Divine Revelation from Vatican II, available at www.vatican.va) for a better understanding of Scripture and divine revelation.

38. Start bringing your Bible to Mass with you.

39. Look up the Holy Father's Wednesday audience online (at www.vatican.va), and read his statement for the week.

40. Read the first two chapters of the Gospel of Luke for a better appreciation of Mary's role in Jesus's life. Consider how you might emulate her willingness to serve.

41. Read *Redemptoris Missio*, Pope John Paul II's Encyclical on the Permanent Validity of the Church's Missionary Mandate (www.vatican.va), for a stronger understanding of the Catholic Church's mission and your role in it.

42. Watch a religious movie about a saint or about an important time in the Church, such as *Paul VI: The Pope in the Tempest*, *For Greater Glory: The True Story of Cristiada*, or *The Passion of the Christ*.

43. Download and read the United States Conference of Catholic Bishops' document *Disciples Called to Witness* (available at www.usccb.org) for a better understanding of the New Evangelization.

44. Get a book on Theology of the Body and read a chapter a week. I recommend *Man and Woman He Created Them: A Theology of the Body* by John Paul II, *Men and Women Are from Eden* by Mary Healy, or *Theology of the Body for Beginners: A Basic Introduction to Pope John Paul II's Sexual Revolution* by Christopher West.

45. Get a copy of *The Rosary Comic Book* by Gene Yang, and pray a rosary while reading it. I promise you, it is one of the greatest rosary books ever published. We have multiple copies in our house, and everyone loves it.

46. Get a better understanding of the Nicene Creed by reading the *Catechism*'s explanation of it (Part I).

47. Get up thirty minutes early every day this week to spend extra

time reading the Bible, the *Catechism*, or some other spiritual work.

48. Find a liturgical calendar, and pay attention to feast days, memorials, and seasons. (Many parishes distribute these in December for the following year.)

49. Learn the meaning behind making the Sign of the Cross.

50. Read a different psalm every day while brushing your teeth.

51. Ask the Holy Spirit for wisdom.

52. Memorize the full genealogy of Jesus Christ in Matthew chapter 1. Just kidding. But, take time to read it. See how many names you recognize from other parts of Scripture—and how many you can actually pronounce. Read them out loud to your friends and coworkers to grow in humility while you're at it.

Fifty-Two Ways to Live Your Faith

1. Pick five garments out of your closet that you haven't worn in a year, and drop them off at St. Vincent de Paul or some other charitable clothing closet.

2. Sit for at least five minutes in front of the tabernacle at your local parish. Tell Jesus you love him, and ask him to help you have a better understanding of the Eucharist.

3. Pray one decade of the rosary.

4. Go to one extra Mass during the week.

5. Go to confession.

6. If you use contraception, ask God to help you understand the Church's teachings about chastity, and pray for his grace to follow them.

7. Invite your priest over for dinner.

8. Tithe. If you don't donate money now, start with just 1 percent of your gross income, then increase it each month. If you already

give 10 percent or more, continue to look for ways to give even more. This is one of the greatest lessons my wife and I have ever learned.

9. When you share a treat with someone else, make sure the other person gets the larger portion.

10. For every canned good you buy this week, buy an extra and donate it to a local food pantry.

11. Make dinner for someone (whether the person is sick or doing fine) and deliver it.

12. Leave the last cookie for someone else. But don't tell anyone you did it.

13. Find a local homeless shelter and offer to help in whatever way is needed: fix meals, clean, or even stay overnight.

14. Do someone else's chores this week in addition to your own.

15. Pray every day for at least one person you know who is going through a difficulty (illness, job, relationship, or whatever).

16. Keep holy water in your house, bless yourself regularly, encourage your children to bless themselves, and bless the rooms in your house.

17. When driving past a Catholic church, keep in mind that Jesus Christ is there in the Eucharist. Bless yourself and call out, "I love you, Jesus!" (If you have kids in the car, you'll be amazed how this becomes habitual for them.)

18. When you hear an emergency siren (ambulance or police), say a Hail Mary or Our Father for the emergency workers and whoever is in need.

19. Move into the middle of the pew at Mass, so that when people show up at the last minute they can find seats.

20. Pray before meals, at home and in public, even if you're by yourself.

21. Learn the parts of the Mass as well as the meanings behind them. Scott Hahn's *The Lamb's Supper: The Mass as Heaven on Earth* is a great start in doing this.

22. Participate in Mass more than ever. Recite the prayers with new fervor. Pay attention to what you're saying.

23. Read the Mass readings (always available at USCCB.org) before going to Mass so you know what to expect.

24. If you know someone who is sick, make the person soup (or buy some good pre-made soup—*not canned*) and deliver it.

25. Make a list of everything in your life that is difficult or bad right now, and then with every ounce of your being, give thanks to God for each and every one of those crosses.

26. Pray for your spouse.

27. Pray a novena for someone.

28. Pray a fifty-four-day novena (three nine-day novenas in petition and three nine-day novenas in thanksgiving), and see how God brings peace into your life.

29. Attend a retreat.

30. Rest on Sunday.

31. Read St. Louis de Montfort's *Preparation for Total Consecration* or Fr. Michael Gaitley's *33 Days to Morning Glory*, and consecrate yourself to Jesus through Mary.

32. Fast. There are different ways to do this. Fast from television for a day. Fast from everything but bread and water for a day. Give up desserts for a week. Make an intentional sacrifice, and offer it up to God.

33. Go on a pilgrimage to a nearby parish. Or if you can afford it, go to the Vatican. (If you're like me, the first one is more realistic.)

34. Place a crucifix above the front door to your home. If you already have one there, get another, and put it above another regularly used door.

35. Keep a modest crucifix on your desk next to your computer keyboard.

36. Don't eat meat on Friday, or make some other sacrificial offering that day in honor of our Lord's Passion.

37. Think of something frivolous in your life that you spend too much time on (playing a certain game, watching dumb movies), and give it up. A few years ago my wife gave me a computer game called Starcraft II, and I loved it. But I soon realized I spent too much time playing it, and it did absolutely nothing to improve my life. So I deleted it and have never regretted it.

38. If you have DVDs, CDs, or books in your house that you wouldn't feel comfortable using if Jesus was sitting right next to you, throw them in the trash.

39. Decide to vote as a Catholic, not as a liberal or conservative.

40. Pray for the pope and the pope's intentions (see ewtn.com for intentions for each month).

41. Always carry a rosary in your pocket or purse, and be ready to pray it at a moment's notice.

42. Don't eat, smoke, chew gum, or drink anything but water for the required one-hour fast before receiving the Eucharist.

43. Pray for vocations. Pray especially for vocations within your family.

44. Show up early for Mass and spend the extra time praying for priests you know, whether you like them or not.

45. Take a shift in a soup kitchen, or volunteer at a parish dinner.

46. Anonymously give cash to someone in need. Put it in an

envelope and drop in the person's mailbox (*after* the mail carrier has arrived for the day), slip it into the person's purse or coat pocket, or find some other creative method of delivery. If you hear of a stranger in need, show up at the person's house, give him or her the money, and then be on your way without an explanation. This actually happened to my wife and me years ago, when I was out of work. To this day I have no idea who that man was who showed up at our front door and handed us an envelope with $1,000 cash inside. I'll never forget it, and I look forward to paying that forward someday.

47. Ask your pastor what ministry needs the most assistance in your parish, and help in whatever way you can.

48. Fill out a commitment card when your parish is doing a stewardship drive.

49. When a school holds a bake sale, always buy something.

50. Make a commitment not to complain all week.

51. Set up a prayer table in a special place in your house with prayer cards, a crucifix, a rosary, a Bible, and other items to facilitate prayer and study.

52. Make a donation to a charitable organization, like Food for the Poor, Catholic Relief Services, or a local Catholic service group.

Fifty-Two Ways to Share Your Faith

1. Start a blog, and write about why you're Catholic.

2. Invite someone to go to Eucharistic Adoration with you.

3. Get a holy card of your favorite saint, and hang it in a modest place in your office or cubicle. If you work from home, tape it to the bathroom mirror. Be ready to tell people (the ones who ask) about this holy person and what he or she means to you.

4. Invite someone (spouse, child, parent, sibling, friend) to pray a decade or whole rosary with you. Offer up that rosary for whoever prays with you.

5. Look through your books about faith, and pick one to give away to someone else.

6. Take your kids to confession, or invite someone else to go to confession with you.

7. Google *Contraception: Why Not?* by Dr. Janet Smith, purchase an MP3 or CD of the talk, listen to it, and then pass it on to someone else.

8. Request a free copy (or purchase multiple copies) of *That Catholic Show* from www.NewEvangelizers.com, and give it to someone who would enjoy it.

9. Start a podcast, and talk about your faith and how it impacts your life. Even if no one subscribes to it, maybe someday your kids will hear it and be inspired.

10. Pray the rosary in a public place. Don't make a show of it, but casually holding a rosary while silently saying prayers can be a powerful witness.

11. Participate in a pro-life demonstration, pray outside an abortion clinic, and show the joy of the pro-life movement in your conversations with others.

12. Show compassion for people with same-sex attraction, and pray for them. Don't condone homosexual behavior, but live out what the Church teaches in the *Catechism*:

> ...[M]en and women who have deep-seated homosexual tendencies...must be accepted with respect, compassion, and sensitivity. Every sign of unjust discrimination in their regard should be avoided. These persons are called to

fulfill God's will in their lives and, if they are Christians, to unite to the sacrifice of the Lord's Cross the difficulties they may encounter from their condition. (*CCC*, 2358; see *CCC*, 2357, 2359)

13. Forgive someone who has hurt you. If possible, let the person know of your forgiveness, especially if he or she has apologized.

14. Ask for forgiveness of anyone you've wronged.

15. Invite a friend to Mass.

16. Invite a friend to a dinner or other event at your parish.

17. Pray with your spouse. If you have difficulty praying out loud with someone else, ask your spouse to lead.

18. When someone of another faith asks you to pray with him or her, do so gladly.

19. Dress for Mass as if you realize that you've been invited to the Eucharistic feast, the Supper of the Lamb, a banquet with Jesus Christ himself. How you dress for dinner with the King of kings and Lord of lords may cause others to realize the importance of each Mass.

20. If you are in a state of mortal sin (having missed Sunday Mass, having used contraception, or for some other serious reason), refrain from receiving the Eucharist until you go to confession. Don't be embarrassed as others pass by. Take solace in the fact that you are witnessing to the importance of the Eucharist by not receiving unworthily (see 1 Corinthians 11:27).

21. Buy Catholic newspaper and magazine subscriptions for other people.

22. Post a Catholic bumper sticker on your car.

23. If you have small children, always give them a dollar to drop in the collection basket, even if you're already tithing over 10 percent.

24. If you have older children, encourage them to give 10 percent of their allowances or earnings to your parish or a charity of their choosing.

25. Pray with your children before bedtime.

26. Eat dinner as a family.

27. Make a video explaining why you love being Catholic, and offer it to family, to friends, and even online.

28. Stay until the very end of Mass, and as you leave refrain from conversation in respect for those still in prayer. If someone tries to engage you in conversation on the way out, smile and simply say, "Let's move out of the church first."

29. Look for Catholic videos on YouTube, and when you find a good one, leave an online comment for the creator. Then forward the link to other people.

30. If someone ever notices your rosary and says something about it, give it to that person immediately. You can learn how to make all-twine knotted rosaries to give away at http://RosaryArmy. NewEvangelizers.com.

31. Offer to teach a class in your parish.

32. Positively comment on people's blogs and other online sites. Don't post anything negative.

33. Encourage and compliment someone in your family who might be going through a tough time.

34. Hang a piece of religious art somewhere prominent in your home.

35. Wear a Catholic T-shirt one day. (Some of my favorite Catholic T-shirts come from http://agnusgiftshop.com.)

36. Ask someone what his or her favorite Bible story is.

37. Volunteer to work on a retreat for adults or teens, either as

a speaker, coordinator, part of the cleanup crew, or whatever is needed.

38. Add a Bible verse or meaningful spiritual quote to the signature on your e-mail account, or add links to useful resources that you'd like to share. Be subtle. Just put the information there, and trust the Holy Spirit to prompt people to click on the links.

39. Arrange to have a Mass offered for someone who is in need, and send a Mass card to let the person know, even if he or she is not Catholic.

40. When someone asks you what you did over the weekend, make sure to tell them you went to Mass.

41. Buy individual copies of an inexpensive book of Catholic prayers for each member of your household.

42. If you know of someone in the hospital or a prison, call your priest and ask him to make a visit. And make a visit yourself.

43. Use Twitter or Facebook to share your favorite verse from this past Sunday's Mass readings.

44. Invite two or three friends to get together for a cup of coffee and to pray together.

45. Get a Catholic board game like Scattergories: Catholic Edition and play it with friends or family. Our kids love Apples to Apples: Bible Edition.

46. Invite some friends over for a beer, and serve them Trappist beer, made by monks.

47. Buy some religious articles like crucifixes, rosaries, and prayer cards, and give them to your pastor to share with others as he sees fit.

48. When going through a drive-through, pay for the person in the car behind you. Then tell the cashier, "God bless you."

The person who receives the food might consider you just a kind person, but the cashier will know you're a Christian.

49. If you work outside the house, get a coffee mug that's clearly Catholic. If anyone asks about it, be ready with a kind explanation.

50. Make sure every person in your house has a Bible, and conduct a mini Bible study.

51. Text an encouraging passage of Scripture to a friend or a family member.

52. Stand up for your faith and morals. Don't swear, even if others do. Don't get drunk, even if your coworkers do. Be a Christian in every situation.

Questions

1. From the lists of ways to know, live, and share your faith, which suggestions jumped out and excited you? Which do you think you could incorporate into your life in the next seven days?

2. Which suggestions made you nervous or uneasy? Why do you think you reacted that way?

3. Was there an item from any of the lists that you think you'd like to make a regular part of your life?

Prayer for Discernment

Lord,

there are so many ways to know my faith, live my faith, and share my faith.

Please help me to discern the *best* way to do each of these, according to your will.

Thank you for entrusting me with such an amazing challenge and worthwhile opportunity.

Amen.

chapter eleven

A Blueprint for Evangelization

> It is time to open the doors and to proclaim again the
> Resurrection of Christ, of which we are witnesses.
> —ARCHBISHOP SALVATORE FISICHELLA, President of the
> Pontifical Council for New Evangelization[1]

In his document *Evangelii Nuntiandi* (On Evangelization in
the Modern World), Pope Paul VI stated "three burning questions" that must be asked in determining how to share the salvific
message of Jesus Christ with the world:

1   In our day, what has happened to that hidden energy
of the Good News, which is able to have a powerful effect
on man's conscience?
2. To what extent and in what way is that evangelical
force capable of really transforming the people of this
century?
3. What methods should be followed in order that the
power of the Gospel may have its effect?[2]

These questions give rise to another: Is today's Church as a whole
capable of answering these questions?

I believe that this is, in part, where the Pontifical Council for the
New Evangelization comes into play. In announcing this council

on June 28, 2010, the Feast of Sts. Peter and Paul, Pope Benedict XVI stated:

> There are regions in the world that still wait for a first evangelization; others that received it but need more profound work; others still in which the Gospel put down roots a long time ago, giving place to a true Christian tradition, but where in the last centuries—with complex dynamics—the process of secularization has produced a grave crisis of the sense of the Christian faith and of belonging to the Church.[3]

The Pontifical Council for the New Evangelization owns

> the specific task of promoting a renewed evangelization in countries where the first proclamation of the faith already resounded and where Churches are present of ancient foundation, but which are going through a progressive secularization of society and a sort of "eclipse of the sense of God."[4]

The work of the council and of the synod of bishops with its focus on the New Evangelization, leading up to the Year of Faith that was launched in October 2012—all indicate a Church that is identifying the challenges facing Catholicism in today's world and meeting those challenges with an attitude of opportunity.

The Year of Faith

One of the most important efforts to encourage people in the New Evangelization is the declaration of a Year of Faith in the Church from October 11, 2012, to November 24, 2013. Not the first Year of Faith the Church has declared, this one was initiated as a "summons to an authentic and renewed conversion to the Lord, the one Savior of the world."[5]

The Year of Faith coincided with both the fiftieth anniversary of the opening of the Second Vatican Council and the twentieth anniversary of the promulgation of the *Catechism of the Catholic Church*. The specific goal set forth in Pope Benedict's *Motu Proprio Data Porta Fidei* is to study and reflect on the sixteen documents that were produced through the Second Vatican Council as well as on the *Catechism*.

It is absolutely necessary to stress that this Year of Faith is meant to be not an event that comes and goes but a catalyst for continued celebration of our faith. Our hope is that the fruits of the Year of Faith, the synod of bishops, the statements from Church leaders and experts, and other efforts focused on the New Evangelization will be lived on a perpetual and ongoing basis. "The 'door of faith' (Acts 14:27) is always open for us," Pope Benedict wrote in *Porta Fidei*, "ushering us into the life of communion with God and offering entry into his Church."[6]

In studying the *Catechism* and the Vatican II documents—through the many books, articles, talks, and online sources that have appeared—we must keep in mind this goal: not just an increase in knowledge but a transformation of our very lives. "It is possible to cross that threshold when the word of God is proclaimed and the heart allows itself to be shaped by transforming grace."[7]

We must be consistently open to the transformation that Jesus can bring to our lives, so that we might experience the joy that he alone can offer. No matter our state of life, our age, our occupation, our education, or our experience; no matter the fractures we've experienced in our personal relationships with other people—in marriage, family, society, or friendships—we are never abandoned by Jesus Christ. He will always welcome us into the arms of the Father.

When speaking to the plenary session of the Congregation for the Doctrine of the Faith in early 2012, Pope Benedict XVI said, "We are facing a profound crisis of faith, a loss of the religious sense that represents the greatest challenge to the Church today."[8]

The New Evangelization is the solution to this crisis. In fact, Pope Benedict XVI has repeated with urgency the message of previous popes: "The renewal of faith must therefore take priority in the commitment of the entire Church in our time."[9]

New Evangelizers in Action: CatholicMom.com's Lisa Hendey

"I love sharing my faith," says Lisa Hendey. "My biggest challenge is doing so in a way that respects those with differing perspectives."

One way Lisa does this is through online evangelization.

In 2000 Lisa founded www.CatholicMom.com as a direct response to Pope John Paul II's invitation to be a part of the New Evangelization.

"Over the years, the site has made use of emerging technology to share the Good News of the gospel," Lisa explains. "From a static website to blog format, from podcasting to the use of social media, I've attempted to connect with Catholics and others who are interested in learning more about the faith."

Her efforts have not only had a positive impact on the regular visitors to Lisa's website, they have provided Lisa with opportunities to serve the Church in unexpected ways—including attendance at the Vatican Bloggers Meeting in 2011, as well as participation in both the 2012 USCCB Bishops and Bloggers Meeting and the Catholic Press

Association press tour of Israel as a guest of the Israeli Ministry of Tourism.

"I was able to share these experiences broadly thanks to social media tools," Lisa says.

In addition to her worldwide ministry online and in print, Lisa also seeks to serve her local parish community through her position as parish webmaster at St. Anthony of Padua Catholic Church in the Diocese of Fresno, as well as participating in other initiatives within her diocese.

Despite heavy involvement in the Church, for Lisa the continued need to develop greater knowledge of Catholicism is ever present.

"As a 'cradle Catholic' catechized in the early years after Vatican II, my faith education in school did not really involve mastery of the *Catechism*, Church documents, or even much history of the Church," says Lisa. "As an adult, I find myself sometimes playing 'catch up' on official Church teachings. I have never doubted my faith in any way, but I do often find deficits in my knowledge of Church teachings. Blessedly, with the help of the Internet it is increasingly simpler to learn these precepts."

The opportunity to keep learning is one of Lisa's biggest goals in the New Evangelization. "I hope to grow in my own faith—in my knowledge of the precepts of the Church, her history, and the truth we find in the *Catechism* and profess in the Creed," Lisa says. "I also hope to do a better job within my domestic Church of being a spiritual light for my family. I hope to provide as many resources as possible for our CatholicMom.com readers to help them to know, love, and share the faith in their homes and communities."

In addition to running CatholicMom.com, Lisa is also the author of *A Book of Saints for Catholic Moms: 52 Companions for Your Heart, Mind, Body, and Soul* and *The Handbook for Catholic Moms: Nurturing Your Heart, Mind, Body, and Soul.*

A New Enthusiasm

So how do we make this a priority? What must we do to counteract the "increasingly widespread opinion that truth is not accessible to man; hence it is necessary to limit oneself to finding rules for a praxis that can better the world"?[10]

It is the need to answer questions such as these that prompted the pope to form the Pontifical Council for the New Evangelization. Shortly thereafter the Holy Father named Archbishop Salvatore Fisichella as the president of this new Vatican dicastery, giving him the charge of initiating a response, to re-propose and bring new life to the faith in today's world. Archbishop Fisichella then stated, "It is time to open the doors and to proclaim again the Resurrection of Christ, of which we are witnesses."[11]

Archbishop Fisichella went on to prioritize the areas on which the Pontifical Council for the New Evangelization will focus, specifically "liturgy, the sacrament of confession, the Eucharist, family, culture, political and civil commitment, immigration, and communication."[12] To truly address each of these areas would require volumes of books. In this book I hope I've imparted to you the foundations of what needs to be done and what your role can be.

At its roots the New Evangelization is developing new methodologies for delivering an ancient message. It is, as Archbishop

Fisichella stated, "a new work, a new language, a new enthusiasm for announcing the Gospel."[13] During the 2012 synod of bishops, he emphasized that the first work to be accomplished in the New Evangelization is the work on ourselves:

> It is urgent that before "doing," the foundation of our "being" Christian is rediscovered so that the New Evangelization is not experienced as an addition in a moment of crisis, but as a continuous mission of the Church.[14]

This is, again, a reminder of the need to know the faith in order to properly live and share the faith. All three of these areas—knowing, living, and sharing—are not one-time, passing moments but areas of constant improvement and transformation.

"Christian life is defined by an encounter with Jesus," stated Cardinal Wuerl at the 2012 synod. "We need to be able, with lively faith, firm conviction and joyful witness, to renew our proclamation with the understanding that as God spoke to us in times past, so does he continue to speak to us today." [15]

To keep in mind this ongoing effort, the synod fathers (the bishops and priests who attended the meeting of bishops) proposed, in particular, that we as Catholics reflect on the Gospel passage of the Samaritan woman at the well and her encounter with Jesus Christ (see John 4:5–42). In many ways, said the bishops, we are all like that woman who stood with her empty bucket at the well. Jesus saw deep into her heart and gave her a drink from a well that would satisfy her thirst for truth. Jesus offers that drink to each of us.

Today's Mission

"I was raised—as were most of you—to think of the missions as 'way far away'—and, to be sure, we can never forget our sacred duty to the foreign missions," wrote Cardinal Timothy M. Dolan of New York. "But, we are a mission territory, too. Every diocese is. And every committed Catholic is a missionary. This is at the heart of what Blessed John Paul II and Pope Benedict XVI call the New Evangelization."[16]

In today's world, ravaged with secularism and relativism and a thousand temptations that divert our focus away from Jesus Christ and his one, holy, catholic, and apostolic Church, "we must," the synod of bishops stated, "discern in order to avoid polluted waters. We must orient the search well, so as not to fall prey to disappointment, which can be damaging."[17]

We orient ourselves toward Jesus Christ in every effort we make to truly know him. For to know Jesus is to know our faith. The same holds true in our every effort to live for him and to share with others our encounter and relationship with him.

Cardinal Wuerl pointed out the areas on which bishops and laypeople need to focus in order to truly facilitate that ongoing transformation. Many of these we've covered throughout this book:

- what or who it is we proclaim—the Word of God
- resources to help us in our task
- elements of the New Evangelization
- some theological principles for the New Evangelization
- qualities of the New Evangelizers.[18]

But what about our unworthiness? What about our sinfulness?

Again looking at the woman at the well, the synod reminds us that, "the sinner who was converted becomes a messenger of salvation and leads the whole city to Jesus."[19] In the same way, our baptism and ongoing repentance lead us to become messengers of salvation for Christ. While there are wide and varied forms that the delivery of that message takes, at the root of it all is our own personal encounter with Christ.

The Church is where that encounter happens.

> The Church is the space offered by Christ in history where we can encounter him, because he entrusted to her his Word, the Baptism that makes us God's children, his Body and his Blood, the grace of forgiveness of sins above all in the sacrament of Reconciliation, the experience of communion that reflects the very mystery of the Holy Trinity, the strength of the Spirit that generates charity towards all.[20]

While the main focus of the synod was the ongoing methods to revive faith in today's world, all efforts in the New Evangelization must be distilled to a single point: Jesus Christ. The Church confirms time and again "that to evangelize one must be evangelized first of all, and sends out a plea—starting with herself—for conversion, because the weaknesses of Jesus's disciples weigh upon the credibility of the mission."[21]

We encounter Jesus through the Church, through the sacraments, through the communion of all believers in receiving Jesus Christ—Body, Blood, soul, and divinity—into their lives. "It is necessary that the sleeping giant, which is the parish, awake! A dynamic parish, charged with the love of God, which fascinates its faithful and challenges them to evangelization, is possible."[22]

In the face of the obstacles that seem to be growing at an exponential rate—in the forms of secularism, relativism, and animosity toward Christ and his Church—we must find new ways of delivering the timeless message that truth is truth and that truth can be found in the person of Jesus Christ.

As Archbishop Salvatore Fisichella stated, "It is time to open the doors and to proclaim again the Resurrection of Christ, of which we are witnesses."[23]

Called to Evangelize

On its website, the United States Conference of Catholic Bishops provides a list of seven key themes that explain the importance of the New Evangelization to Catholics:[24]

1. The New Evangelization is not new in content but new in energy and approach.
2. It begins with personal conversion.
3. It applies to believers and non-believers alike.
4. The New Evangelization is about our own personal encounter with Jesus Christ.
5. It's not just an event but an ongoing mission.
6. It is meant to be a faith-based answer to a culture being swallowed by secularism.
7. It's a priority for the Church.

Let's keep these themes in mind and apply them to our daily actions. We will be disciples called to witness, and we will effect dramatic change in this world.

This is what you've been called to: You have been called to be a disciple. You have been called to be open to the Holy Spirit working through you, to draw you and those you encounter into a deeper relationship with Jesus Christ. You have been called to proclaim the Good News of salvation offered by our Messiah and King. You have been called to be a New Evangelizer.

In our various efforts of service, our ministries and apostolates, our parishes and communities, when we work in communion and conjunction and cooperation with the Holy Spirit, we fulfill our duty as disciples called to witness. We become New Evangelizers, new messengers, of an eternal message of hope, joy, and redemption.

Questions

1. How will you know your faith more completely a week from now?
2. How will you be living your faith more fully a week from now?
3. How will you be sharing your faith more successfully a week from now?
4. If you're still intimidated by the idea of taking a role in the New Evangelization, what are some concrete steps you can take to begin the process of overcoming that fear?

Prayer for Inspiration

Lord,
there might be times when my enthusiasm for knowing,
living, and sharing my faith outweighs my actions.
In those times, Lord, inspire me.
Help me to see clearly your will for my life.
Help me to see clearly my role in the New Evangelization.
Inspire me, Lord, to know you more today.

Inspire me, Lord, to live for you more today.

Inspire me, Lord, to share my faith in you more today.

I offer myself, through the intercession of our Blessed Mother,

to be at your service in the New Evangelization.

Amen.

Notes

A Short Chapter (Introduction)

1. Cardinal Timothy Dolan, "*Missio ad gentes* and New Evangelization," address during the Day of Prayer and Reflection of the College of Cardinals the day before the consistory creating twenty-two new cardinals, as reported by Vatican Radio, February 17, 2012, www.news.va.

2. Cardinal Donald Wuerl, Report at the Synod of Bishops, "New Evangelization Is the Re-Introduction, the Re-Proposing, of Christ," October 9, 2012, www.zenit.org.

Chapter One: *Who, Me?*

1. Pope John Paul II, Homily for Inauguration of Pontificate, 5, October 22, 1978, www.vatican.va.

2. Pope John Paul II, *Crossing the Threshold of Hope*, Vittorio Messori, ed., Jenny McPhee and Martha McPhee, trans. (New York: Alfred A. Knopf, 1994), p. 219.

Chapter Two: *Defining the New Evangelization*

1. Nelson Mandela, quoted in Peter Coleman, *The Five Percent: Finding Solutions to Seemingly Impossible Conflicts* (New York: PublicAffairs, 2011), p. 218.

2. John Paul II, Homily at the Shrine of the Holy Cross, 1, Mogila, Poland, June 9, 1979, www.vatican.va.

3. Pope John Paul II, *Veritatis Splendor*, Encyclical on the Splendor of Truth, 109, August 6, 1993, quoting Congregation for the Doctrine of the Faith, Instruction on the Ecclesial Vocation of the Theologian *Donum Veritatis* (May 24, 1990), 6, www.vatican.va.

4. Pope John Paul II, *Redemptoris Missio*, Encyclical on the Permanent Validity of the Church's Missionary Mandate, 42, December 7, 1990, www.vatican.va.

5. Pope John Paul II, *Redemptoris Missio*, 43.

6. United States Conference of Catholic Bishops, *Disciples Called to Witness*, Preface, third paragraph, www.usccb.org.

7. Pope John Paul II, *Redemptoris Missio*, 33.

8. Pope John Paul II, *Redemptoris Missio*, 86.
9. Pope Benedict XVI, Address to New Council on Evangelization, May 30, 2011, www.vatican.va.

Chapter Three: *Don't Be Squishy*

1. Pope Benedict XVI, address to newly appointed bishops, as quoted by Vatican Radio, September 20, 2012, www.news.va.
2. Dolan, "*Missio ad gentes* and New Evangelization."
3. *Instrumentum Laboris*, "The New Evangelization for the Transmission of the Christian Faith," 164, May 27, 2012, www.vatican.va.
4. Dolan, "*Missio ad gentes* and New Evangelization."
5. Pope Benedict XVI to new bishops.
6. Pope Benedict XVI, Address to Participants in the Plenary Assembly of the Pontifical Council for Culture, March 8, 2008, www.vatican.va.
7. Pope Benedict XVI, to the Plenary Assembly of the Pontifical Council for Culture.
8. Homily of Cardinal Joseph Ratzinger, April 18, 2005, www.vatican.va.

Chapter Four: *Deserts and Dark Nights*

1. Pope Paul VI, Address to the College of Cardinals, June 22, 1973, as quoted in *Evangelii Nuntiandi*, Apostolic Exhortation on Evangelization in the Modern World, 3, December 8, 1975, www.papalencyclicals.net.
2. David Mrazek, M.D., "Antidepressant Use Soaring Among Americans 12 and Over," December 7, 2011, www.mayoclinic.com.
3. Pope Benedict XVI, Homily at the Beginning of His Petrine Ministry as Bishop of Rome, April 24, 2005, www.vatican.va.
4. See Brian Kolodiejchuk, ed., *Mother Teresa: Come Be My Light* (New York: Doubleday, 2007).
5. John of the Cross, *Dark Night of the Soul*, E. Allison Peers, trans. (New York: Image, 1990), p. 44.

Chapter Five: *Why Sheep Get Lost*

1. Albert Einstein, as quoted in Jerome Pohlen, *Albert Einstein and Relativity for Kids: His Life and Ideas with 21 Activities and Thought Experiments* (Chicago: Chicago Review, 2012), p. 110.
2. A Gallup Survey of Catholics Regarding Holy Communion, January

1992, revealed that only 30 percent of Roman Catholics hold an accurate view of Holy Communion. In addition to the 30 percent who consider the Eucharist to be a symbol of Jesus, about 40 percent hold some other non-Catholic belief. www.traditio.com.

Center for Applied Research in the Apostolate (CARA), "Sacraments Belief and Practice Among U.S. Catholics," http://cara.george-lu.

"Sacraments Today," Also cited in *Disciples Called to Witness*,

: *A Basic Definition of Catholicism*

ling to a report commissioned by the Pew Forum from the Center Study of Global Christianity (CSGC) at Gordon-Conwell, about ne thousand Christian organizations currently exist worldwide. ppendix B: Methodology for Estimating Christian Movements," www.pewforum.org. A footnote stipulates that "this is the global sum of the total number of denominations in each country. There is overlap between countries because many denominations are present in more than one country." I think it's pretty safe to say that there are at least five thousand denominations.

2. *Lumen Gentium*, Dogmatic Constitution on the Church, 13, in Austin Flannery, ed., *Vatican Council II, Volume 1: The Conciliar and Post Conciliar Documents* (New York: Costello, 1998), pp. 364–365; see John 11:52.

3. George Santayana, *Reason in Common Sense*, vol. 1, *The Life of Reason* (New York: Dover, 1980), chap. 12, www.gutenberg.org.

4. Janet Smith, *Contraception, Why Not?* available through janetesmith. org.

Chapter Seven: *Accepting the Mission*

1. Catholic Answers, "Is Catholicism Pagan?" This and other tracts are available at www.catholic.com.

2. Ann Schneible, "Fulfilling the Call to Evangelize," April 8, 2012, www. zenit.org.

3. "Archbishop Salvatore Fisichella's Intervention at the Synod of Bishops," October 10, 2012, www.zenit.org.

4. Pope John Paul II, *Redemptoris Missio*, 23.

5. See www.austindiocese.org.

Chapter Eight: *Becoming a New Evangelizer*

1. Phyllis Theroux, as quoted on numerous online sites.

2. Pope John Paul II, *Novo Millennio Ineunte*, January 6, 2001, 40, www.vatican.va.

Chapter Nine: *Twenty-First-Century Fishing Tips*

1. Augustine, *City of God*, bk. 15, chap. 1, in Philip Schaff, ed., *St. Augustine's City of God and Christian Doctrine*, vol. 2, *Nicene and Post-Nicene Fathers, Series 1* (Grand Rapids: Eerdmans, 2009), www.ccel.org.

Chapter Eleven: *A Blueprint for Evangelization*

1. Archbishop Salvatore Fisichella, at a gathering of bishops, priests, and lay people in Rome, October 15, 2011, as quoted by Antonio Gaspari, "A Giant Is Awakening: New Evangelization Flows Out of Rome," www.zenit.org, October 18, 2011.

2. Pope Paul VI, *Evangelii Nuntiandi*, Apostolic Exhortation on Evangelization in the Modern World, 4, December 8, 1975, www.papalencyclicals.net.

3. Pope Benedict XVI, Homily at Vespers for Sts. Peter and Paul, "The Church Is an Immense Force of Renewal in the World," June 28, 2010, www.zenit.org.

4. Pope Benedict XVI, Homily at Vespers for Sts. Peter and Paul.

5. Pope Benedict XVI, Apostolic Letter *Motu Proprio Data Porta Fidei* for the Indiction of the Year of Faith, 6, October 11, 2011, www.vatican.va.

6. Pope Benedict XVI, *Porta Fidei*, 1.

7. Pope Benedict XVI, *Porta Fidei*, 1.

8. Pope Benedict XVI, Address to Participants in the Plenary Meeting of the Congregation for the Doctrine of the Faith, January 27, 2012, www.vatican.va.

9. Pope Benedict XVI, Address to the Plenary Meeting of the Congregation for the Doctrine of the Faith.

10. Pope Benedict XVI, Address to the Plenary Meeting of the Congregation for the Doctrine of the Faith.

11. Archbishop Fisichella, as quoted in Gaspari.

12. Gaspari.

13. Archbishop Fisichella, as quoted in Jim Lackey, "The New Evangelization, Explained," April 11, 2012, Catholic News Service Blog, cnsblog.wordpress.com.

14. Archbishop Salvatore Fisichella, Intervention at the Synod of Bishops, October 10, 2012, www.zenit.org.

15. Cardinal Wuerl, Report at the Synod of Bishops.

16. Cardinal Timothy Dolan, "Gospel in the Digital Age" blog, July 17, 2012, as quoted in "Cardinal Dolan Sees US as 'Mission Territory,'" July 18, 2012, Catholicnewsagency.com.

17. *Instrumentum Laboris.*

18. Cardinal Wuerl, Report at the Synod of Bishops.

19. *Instrumentum Laboris.*

20. *Instrumentum Laboris.*

21. Holy See Press Office, "Official Summary of the Year of Faith," October 26, 2012, www.zenit.org.

22. Don Gigi Perini, a parish priest of Milan, as quoted in Gaspari.

23. Archbishop Fisichella, as quoted in Gaspari.

24. Peter Murphy, "7 Keys to New Evangelization," *The Georgia Bulletin,* October 25, 2012, www.georgiabulletin.org.

About the Author

Greg Willits is the director of Evangelization and Family Life Ministries for the Archdiocese of Denver. He is the cofounder of New Evangelizers, Rosary Army, *That Catholic Show,* and several other apostolates dedicated to helping people grow in their faith. He is also the former president and COO of the Star Quest Production Network (SQPN.com), and is responsible for organizing the first Catholic New Media Conference, which annually continues to bring together bloggers, podcasters, and others working in new media from around the world. He and his wife, Jennifer, are the coauthors of *The Catholics Next Door: Adventures in Imperfect Living,* and together they are the parents of four sons and a daughter. You can visit him online at www. NewEvangelizers.com and www.GregWillits.com.

Follow Greg Online:
    www.GregWillits.com—Speaking, writing, and new media
    www.NewEvangelizers.com—Tools and resources for the New Evangelization
Twitter:
    @Gregwillits—Personal
    @NewEvangelizers—New Evangelizers
Facebook:
    Facebook.com/NewEvangelizers
    Facebook.com/TheCatholicsNextDoor
    Facebook.com/RosaryArmy
Podcast:
    TheCatholicsNextDoor.NewEvangelizers.com/show/